An Idiot's Guide to

a Drink Free

Christmas

A Memoir

Kevin O'Sullivan

For all the dogs

An Idiot's Guide to a Drink Free Christmas

I wrote diaries in my youth.

The writing flowed, and the folly of youth allowed me to believe that what I was writing was somehow important. I remained blissfully unembarrassed by the streams of gobbledygook that flowed from my adolescent pen.

For my pen was also a mere youth, but alas! His ink has long ago run dry, as has the oodles of creativity that once ran through my veins. I now find myself restricted. I am afraid to write what I feel as I suspect that I may in fact feel nothing, and anything I may write may just illustrate that my supposedly matured mind has nothing going on in it at all! But there is still something very special about being in possession of a brand new, pristine, and thus far unadulterated diary. The feel of the pen as it undulates its way through the first page is second to none, it being both nostalgic and suggestive of future possibilities.

This shall be my book. This shall be one of the things I resolved to do this year, and I hereby declare to remain loyal to it regardless of the literary crimes that I will undoubtedly commit.

I am only on the second page but already my beloved book is showing signs of returning my promised commitment to it.

I find myself in Shannon Airport's departure lounge, on the 23rd of December 2012. I have a long wait until my boarding time, and in the dim and not so distant past I would be

1

busying myself with as much imbication of alcoholic beverages as is humanly possible, in an obviously futile attempt to deaden the drudgery of travelling. I would have had at least two pints and a couple of chasers in the time it has taken me to write up to this point, and I would have invariably ended up squashed into those airborne tubes of toothpaste that pass for airplanes these days with an unbearable desire to relieve myself. Squirming frantically, even as the winged carton of Colgate prepares to taxi its way to the runway. So this little endeavour has already spared me that ordeal and the distraction it provides from all that lovely gargle at the bar is most welcome, even if it has left me feeling totally and utterly drained after a mere two pages.

4 Days Later.

Is It possible to live an entire lifetime in four days? "No" I hear you say?

Not unless you pop off to meet your maker after a mere 96 hours, as any a poor crater has done.

Well, I beg to differ, as I believe I have just done so.

It was a lifetime of travelling on British motorways in the pouring rain. My wellbeing, my very destiny entrusted to family members who have had my motorised travel facilitation forced upon them. It was a lifetime of being agog at the wonders of young life displayed by Ci-Ci, my two year old niece, who lives an entire lifetime every day. Two days spent in the house of the Cornwall Joneses, my niece and her husband, this year's short straw drawers who had a very large, and very dull, stray Irish waif descend upon them, and proceeded to be the most gracious, patient, tolerant and accommodating hosts in all of Christendom. I must one day find an independent path, and cease to impose myself upon whoever will have me at Christmas. Failing this, I will take up permanent Yuletide residence on Easter Island, where I will party with the statues in the glorious realisation that the red-clad demon who is Santa Claus shall pass us all by.

Not that I dislike Christmas per se, it has its uses. Time off work is very welcome, and it is a magnificent time for children, as my astounding grand-niece has just so beautifully demonstrated. I fear however, that I am no longer a child, and my time off work is often spent wishing I had something productive to do.

I am now in Somerset with my sister and remarkably cute Yorkshire terrier, a little chap called Murphy.

I can feel completely relaxed here, as my sister and I are twins. We were born 15 months apart back in the swinging sixties, but that is a trifling detail. In every other respect we are twins, and we think in a sort of synchronised telepathic symmetry. I wasn't surprised, in fact, to find out yesterday that we both have difficulty dealing with the atrocities perpetrated by various parties during the second world war. A peculiar kind of guilt complex in my case, and an overwhelming sense of horror at what unfolded all those years ago for us both.

Laughing is not permitted here as a heavy chest infection has rendered my unfortunate sister incapable of experiencing

3

mirth, with is a difficult situation as every word I utter is generally received with utter hilarity. Time is generally spent watching Columbo re-runs, playing with Murphy and indulging in our great shared passion – that which is SCRABBLE^{tm}. Murphy is a particularly talented football player, which provides us with our requisite indoor exercise.

Typically, I flew into the wrong airport, and I am now extremely concerned that I may not get back there in time to return to dear old Ireland. Another marathon perambulation along one of England's grisly motorways is inevitable, my fate once more dependent on a long suffering sibling. Karen assures me it will all be fine, and I must put my faith in her ever enduring optimism, despite the fact that her motor car is in frighteningly fragile condition. It appears that it too has a severe chest infection that produces strange rattling and wheezing sounds, akin to a Tasmanian devil's death throes.

Thus far, not a drop of intoxicating beverage has passed my lips, which has been a uniquely intoxicating experience in itself. I even turned down two bottles of very exotic looking beer, offered to me as a Christmas gift by my kind host's mother down in Cornwall. An unexpected occurrence, worthy of inclusion in any respectable annals!

To be quite frank, things are complicated enough without adding a hangover to the mix, and abstinence is eminently achievable with a minimum of effort. I am a great lover of beer, particularly Guinness, and I have the ability to imbibe gargantuan amounts in one sitting. While others are falling in stupefied heaps all around me, I am clicking my fingers at the bar staff in gleeful anticipation of more. Heavy drinking is a natural consequence of being Irish. It is the done thing, the most abnormal of social norms, and if you are not participating in our great national pastime, you are in danger of becoming socially isolated. The cultivation of a healthy regard for oneself becomes indispensable, but happily, the longer sobriety persists the greater ones contentment with oneself becomes, if you will excuse my French.

I gave up drinking entirely by accident, the week before the Easter weekend, all of nine months ago, was the last time I cut a forlorn figure, propping up the bar of my former local, desperately trying to engage in a meaningful conversation with someone (anyone!) as I made myself sicker and sadder with every perfunctory vessel of soul destroying poison. So I went through the motions, convincing myself that there was a greater social purpose to what I was doing, a sense of loyalty to the very people who constantly busied themselves with avoiding engagement with me at all costs, drinking my fill and sleeping it off, before suffering unbearably through another working week, quite unable to shake off the alcohol's residual effects.

But something must have occurred deep within my subconscious mind on that fateful final weekend, as I emerged from it suddenly quite determined to put an end to the cycle of horrors that constitute a social life on the old sod.

The following weekend, my mother was visiting and I forsook my usual imbications.

I walked with my mother along a road in Ennis, in the county of Clare, and a persistent white dog followed us. This is my last clear memory before the blur of abstinence began to cloud my brain. I made no conscious decision to leave and old life style behind, but by some peculiar twist, I found myself embarking on a journey to self-re-discovery, my head began to clear and it soon became apparent that there was a world around me.

I had given up drink by accident, or had drink just given up on me?

Some Days Later

I am propped up in a seat at Gatwick Airport. I consider myself fortunate, both to be at Gatwick Airport, and to be propped up in a seat, as they appear to be at a premium today. I kicked my long suffering sister out of her bed at six this morning, driven by a burning anxiety to be driven to this aeroplane repository, convinced I would be late, and of course I have arrived all of three and a half hours early. It is the 30th of December and exhaustion is the order of the day. My sitting position may also be dictating the quality of my handwriting.

My thoughts are nothing but a collection of jumbled up Scrabble tiles. I have spent the vast majority of my seven day stay here in England on the receiving end of countless Scrabble thrashings at the hands of my merciless sister. Simple mental functions no longer compute.

No! No more I's! Please! Enough! Enough of the dreaded letter **I. I** am cursed by it. Haunted by it, it dogs my every move! The person committing these strangely disjointed thoughts to paper wishes to take a distinctly protracted sabbatical form the Scrabble board. He may begin to refer to himself in the third person in order to avoid repeated employment of the letter '**I**'. He is a barely functioning person, but he will continue to allow his pen to flow over the page in the hope that it develops a literary conscience all of its own and spares this innocent and unsuspecting missal further punishment. He wishes to comment on his Christmas, but he bears a certain resentment toward the entire festival, not least because of its unnaturally frequent reoccurrences and the pressure it places upon a person to abandon his carefully cultivated and well established routine, casting him into a maelstrom of uncertainty and dependency on others.

On this occasion, a peculiar desire, a certain nagging propulsion overtook him. A unbearable need to be somewhere else even before he knew where exactly he was situated. A gnawing rat inhabited the innermost parts of his cranium and began to insist that he go home. *Get thee hither! Return to your place of origin! You do not belong! There is no purpose to your visit! There is no reason for your existence!*

Keep writing in your book!

Become totally engrossed with it, and you will undoubtedly miss your flight announcement as the black hellghoulies prepare to emerge from the cracks between the tiles under your feet and proceed to drag you downwards into ghastly Gatwick cellars where you will be doomed to spend eternity waiting for a plane that cannot fly and staring in abject and forlorn hunger at the throngs of impossibly beautiful females who have already assaulted your senses every time you have looked up from your already doomed diary.

You are no longer the third person, or the second or the first person for that matter, because I am addressing you now, and I have no idea who I am. You tell me I am a cranium gnawing rodent, so a cerebrum devouring gerbil I shall be, I am not the letter I so you can relax a little, but I am here to tell you how you got on at xmas because you are obviously incapable of doing so yourself.

And those were the last words I wrote. Strange to think I was still at the airport then. Uncomfortable though it may be, I am back in the first person for now as I attempt to produce a page from a period of utter nothingness. I think I may have spent the last few days recovering my senses after having had them ripped away from me during our recent travelling terrors.

The plane was delayed so we all huddled together in groups, staring at the monitor. Information for every flight but ours seemed to register before our boggling eyes as we desperately struggled to pass the time with puzzles, diaries and assorted electronic contraptions. I don't believe security could have been any more stringent upon entering that cold and foreboding airport. Every orifice, every nook and cranny was carefully investigated by huge teams of probing operatives upon entry. Not once, but at least three times, a hapless traveller is required to produce passport and boarding pass whilst being clinically scrutinised by hordes of prodding and poking personnel. A commuter is left inevitably harangued by this ordeal upon entry and is always relieved to find solace in a comfy seat upon his release from such torment.

But then they push you too far! Despite the fact that an errant flea could not enter that dreadful hellhole without current ID and a boarding pass, despite check after check, search after bloody humiliating search and measures that entirely eliminate the possibility of entry from unauthorised visitors, you are still required to show your boarding pass when purchasing a sandwich and a tin of fizzy pop at the shop! You must, in fact, root through your blasted bag every time you want to do anything! You can't fart without a boarding pass! An already harassed passenger is very likely to lose it, particularly if he has been up since the crack of dawn and has been heavily involved in yet another Scrabble marathon into the wee small hours before that.

So that is how I ended up on the wrong plane, flying to Paraguay without a notion of what was happening. This is how I ended up banged up abroad, busted for trying to smuggle half a packet of Rennie out of the UK. I have to say, mind you, that this flaming South American prison, with all its gringo hating psycho killers milling about, is like a bloody holiday camp compared to Gatwick Airport during the holiday season.

So, after the Irish ambassador to Peru, Seamus McGillacuddy, kindly intervened, I now find myself back at work. He was going to have my sentence commuted, but I told him I would prefer not to commute anymore. It's a jungle out there folks! I am back at work, I brought my trusty diary with me, and I intend to fill it with a daily dose of nonsense whenever the opportunity arises. I have just been visited at my bench by my friend and colleague, 'The Bishop' Kevin Jones. A finer man and theologian does not exist on this Earth. He brilliantly communicated his experiences of a school reunion that he attended during my absence. It has left me reeling. He listed of a collection of wonderful folk who I have not seen for over 30 years and am now most unlikely to ever see again. I so desperately wanted to attend this get together, but alas, could not. He beautifully recreated our school days with every word he said and I am now suffering an almost terminal dose of nostalgia. My absence was noted, according to the reverend Jones, and that is some small consolation.

And so the dust has settled on another Christmas break. The next one will be along in the blink of an eye, so we had better busy ourselves in preparation for it. I have gotten over my reluctance to write this book. I am now resigned to the fact that I can no longer write coherently, puerile annotated garbage is inevitable, and I shall use words like 'annotated' when I am stuck for a descriptive metaphor, even if I haven't got a clue what they mean. I shall take liberty after liberty with the English language and be damned. I have been around long enough, and written enough unmitigated shite to know that it matters not. This may be for my one amusement, but others are welcome to get involved. I shall endeavour not to denigrate a single living soul, or otherwise, and keep the entire thing controversy free.

Previous experience has tragically demonstrated the truth in the old adage, and the pen can indeed be mightier than the sword. I once found myself high and dry in a Mississippi monsoon having put pen to some unwanted opinions, which were subsequently perused by unintended parties, and ever after all persons included in print have been dealt with with nothing other than absolute adoration.

All peoples are marvellous, and those that are not, of which there are none, shall not be alluded to. I shall create something out of nothing when there is nothing going on, and I shall make nothing out of something if that something is blatantly unpalatable.

The primary purpose of this exercise is to while away unwanted time as we prepare to head back to England to see Karen and Murphy, for although I have just spent time with them, it does not feel that way. It is regrettable to think that I could not quite come to grips with my recent visits to Somerset and Cornwall, and that they passed by almost without registering in my mind. Is this the nature of Christmas? A fleeting flirtation with places and people that passes by so very quickly as we desperately try to get a handle on it? Did those nasty brain rodents eat my experiences even before they entered my consciousness? Did it really happen? Or was it all a dream? The one annual holiday that I ever get to indulge in, the break I desperately seek all year long. It comes. It goes. *But does it really happen?*

Knuckling Down to a New Year

Here we are, Twenty thirteen.

Sounds utterly ridiculous, doesn't it?

I mean to say, it was 1978, I was listening to
Meatloaf warbling about a bat out of Hell, the sun
shone consistently for endless months, I experienced
the pleasures of the flesh for the first time, I
discovered the world around me with great joy. I was
fit, healthy, and full of beans. Football and girls were
all that mattered, and in that order too, as we would
not cavort with those ladies until our day's football
was done. My dear friend Pascal and I would sit at
the boiler, our very special meeting place, and share
our unique view of the world until it came to shape
us, until it began to build the people we became.

It was perfect. The ideal launching pad from which to
send our personages out into the cosmos, capped by
an incredible event, when we witnessed the most
spectacular heavenly happening, a gargantuan
orange comet racing through the sky in front of us.
The trail that it blazed became a symbol of our
enduring friendship right up until this day, and I can
still quite easily recall it in all its glory. The world
stopped. All that had gone before, all the wonders, all

the adolescent exuberance was encapsulated in that magic moment.

But time did not stop. It continued, it carried on for another 35 years and it continues on its relentless path to nowhere as we speak. Or as you say "Bollocks" and I write. We cannot stop it. We cannot go back to the Nirvana of 1978, but it can stop us, and if it does, we shall always have Tola Park, the boiler, all those years ago, when everything made sense, when you could taste the clean air, when mundanity had yet to be invented, when incredible music filled the air, when life had an infectious beat, verses, a melody and a chorus. Before perfection began to fragment, the opposite sex proved to be more complicated than previously thought, the body began to disintegrate, and the path became littered with unexpected obstacles, reality being principle among them.

To say I enjoyed an idyllic childhood would be a frankly criminal understatement. I began life in Shannon when I was ten. Before that I was a little English boy in Crawley, Sussex, enjoying an idyllic childhood. Climbing trees and fishing for minnows in Tilgate Forest, where, incidentally, the world's first dinosaur bones were discovered at the bottom of the very same bomb craters myself and my little mates

Bobby and Geoffrey used to play mock war games in. As a ten year old, moving to Ireland was quite a culture shock, but I adapted quickly, and Shannon was a new town filled with folk from all corners of the Earth.

It was a phenomenal place to grow up. Wide open spaces, dogs everywhere, nothing but footy and fun. The joy was all in the people. An extraordinary cacophony of collective voices. We had no idea at the time, but we were living in a total utopian wonderland. I still consider myself to be one of the luckiest people alive, although the demeanour I developed in subsequent years may not always testify to that fact.

Until my dying day, I shall always be grateful for having had such a time, and having the knowledge of this takes a chunk of the trepidation away from consideration of my aforementioned dying day.

I am grateful for it, but I was not at the time, for I had no concept of it. I took it all for granted, and in the years that followed I lost sight of all the good, I began to wallow in misery of my own creation, I abused my exalted position in this world. My history is littered with regrets brought about by my own ego. My idyll was replaced with idols, drinking and getting bombed on anything going became my principle concern. I was obsessed with some vacant concept of spirituality achieved through total immersion in negativity. I saw something enlightening about complete darkness. The Brendan Behan school of absolute iniquity. A man, I thought, can only be creative while indulging in his own destruction. I forsook the wonders of the world around me and eventually obliterated all positivity from my life. I did this I completed this task. It was done. I achieved it all by myself.

I have no desire to 'Harp' on about the demon drink, but the sobriety I have recently acquired has enabled me to distance myself from my past and the person I was while endured every hellish day of it. I am back in touch with the kid who sat beside Pascal on the boiler. There are many millions of meteorites flying about and another shall come my way.

It may signal an end rather than a beginning, but at least I'll be able to behold it with an uncluttered mind.

My existence is a solitary one, a fact exemplified by the silence that greeted me upon my return from my sister's homely abode, but it is something I have cultivated for myself. Peace, solitude, and the chance to remain in control. No more shall I suffer the consequences of my self-destructive ways, the calamities that befall me in future shall not be of my own making. If solitude is the price I must pay, then so be it. I have lived a hectic life of never ending social interaction. I have had my fill, and require no more.

So here we are, and it appears this diary has begun in earnest. I know it is written with an apparent audience in mind, and I am aware that that audience probably does not actually exist, but I cannot write in any other way.

I cannot simply write a convention diary, as that would consist of this:

> Work, eat, sleep (weekdays.)

> Housework, eat, sleep (weekends.)

Vast tracts of time are spent relieving the tension that comes with being a red blooded male with distinct needs and a lot more time is spent wishing I wasn't cursed with such undeniable evidence of my humanity. This year however, I shall knuckle down to some diet and exercise. So much so, in fact, that my knuckles will be so down as to be dragging along the road, as intend to wear my legs down into little stumps through excessive walking.

That's how I spend the rest of my time. Making plans and having good intentions.

Thursday 3rd Jan.

I have most definitely aged quite considerably since last year!

It may relate to the fact that I got stuck in Karen's bathtub on more than one occasion during my Somerset sojourn and was forced to exit my ceramic trap through the use of my legs and nothing else, flooding my thankfully tolerant sister's house in the process, but my hips are giving me a murderously painful time of it right now, and are beginning to behave in much the same way as my shoulders, which became weakened to such an extent last year as to render them quite incapable of providing he requisite leverage to extricate my gargantuan frame from bathtubs.

My shoulder and arms are much improved and I feel I may be on the verge of a full recovery on that front, but for months last year I experienced quite the most intense pain imaginable every time I tried to move, and was actually on the verge of undergoing operations to try to remedy the situation. But I decided to hold off, which proved to the by far the best decision I have ever made, as the returns to the joints by some natural process and I regain almost full mobility. Further evidence of a guiding light, or intervention from a benign spiritual force.

I am convinced of the presence of a benevolent celestial presence in my life for a myriad of what I consider to be rational and undeniable reasons. I am certain beyond any doubt that this life is a mere stepping stone to another existence, having had incontrovertible evidence of the afterlife presented to me a little over two years ago. I will allude further to this remarkable phenomenon when I feel it is prudent.

It is not something I feel it is prudent to bandy about willy-nilly, as it is quite Earth shattering in its implication, and has, in an instant, changed my entire belief system and instilled in me an entirely new outlook, and a totally transformed perspective on absolutely everything. I believe I am of sound mind, although perusal of this book may cast a doubt in the mind of your good self, the reader. I can assure you, however, that there is no one on this planet who possesses a sounder mind. My mind is so sound, in fact, as to render it altogether predictable, mundane, tedious and beyond mental aberration of any kind. Downright boring, in fact.

So, I feel qualified to continue. I currently reside at 12 Maple House, Shannon, in the county of Clare, Ireland.

It is a flat, or what some people choose to call an apartment in some vague and vacuous attempt to make it sound posher than what it is, which is a flat, by any other name, whatever that means. But I digress! I left a nice little house in 2001 after being resident there for thirteen years , in the belief that I could somehow escape from my past.

But I was quick to learn that you bring memories with you wherever you go, and moving from a solid little house into a ramshackle, unstable, mouldy, manky and decomposing flat was a complete folly, and further evidence, in any were needed, that I am a class 'A' nincompoop. Nicompoopiness prevented me from giving the flat a proper going over before I took the plunge and purchased it from a fella who could barely contain his joy when I said "Alright. I'll give you the full price so long as you throw in that coffee table".

A surveyor I am not. A twit I am, and I was soon to discover that I had bought myself a proper dud. Holes appeared in the ceiling, from which warms of ghastly little black swamp flies proliferated, the plumbing became increasingly unpredictable, streams of black gunk began to cascade down the walls, the origins of which are still a mystery. A combination of damp and dry rot produced a pong that resembled a wombat's underpants, the previous occupant's hastily erected attempts to disguise the malaise were soon tragically exposed as the entire interior began to rapidly implode revealing the true nature of what amounted to a true shithole.

One fateful day, I decided it was time to risk a shower. I stood in the tiny cubicle and turned on the ancient apparatus. A trickle of cold water dribbled out from the apparently medieval shower head, before the customary trickle of unidentifiable gungey matter began to mingle with the Johnsons baby shampoo in y hair. I had almost completed the ordeal when the shower walls fell inward, and to cap it all, the floor collapsed beneath me, showering the flat below with a mixture of concrete debris and forty five years of matted hair.

Needless to say, the chap below became rather irate as he surveyed the debacle above his head. As I was still standing there with my feet precariously perched on the rim of the shower base, one on each side, don't you know, I shudder to this day at the thought of the view that greeted him. His front room was destroyed and my finances suffered terribly as we sorted out the mess. Funnily enough, the insurance people didn't want to know about it, citing some loop-hole or other in their defence.

This calamity occurred only a few months into my occupation and I was to spend the next ten years sitting in a mouldy chair while abject misery invaded every fibre of my being. I tried valiantly on many an occasion to patch things up, spending as fortune on various house improvements, but it was never enough, and I could not hold back the tide of naturally occurring decay that had pervaded every last inch of my living quarters.

I breathed pure mould; the shit was thick in the air. For ten years I sat powerless, cursing the day I sold myself out for a lousy coffee table. "Whatever shall I do?" I used to mutter as I became resigned to life in a living hell. There was simply nothing to be done, that was my lot, and it was probably more than I deserved after a life time of self-indulgence and casual indifference.

Then it happened. The intervention. You might call it fate, or destiny, or simply a dose of good fortune. But I know, beyond argument, that it was something else entirely.

It was Christmas 2010, and I was happily supping cans of ale with Karen and Murphy when the phone rang. A friend got on the blower to impart some terrible news. The flat had been flooded. An unprecedented cold snap reminiscent of the worst excesses of the Antarctic on a particularly cold day had caused the pipes to burst and most of the building had been saturated.

My friend, for reasons best known to himself, had been staying in my gaff for the yuletidinal period that was in it. "I soaked up most of the shit, I was up til five doing it. I fucked all the furniture I could save on to your bed" he kindly informed me. I then became Karen's worth nightmare, a melancholy visitor living in perpetual dread of returning to a world of devastation. Gloom overtook me as I drank myself into a stupefied oblivion for a week before facing up the trip home.

When I got home, it really wasn't as bad as all that. The flat had been in such a sorry state to begin with that it appeared as if this supposedly catastrophic flood had actually improved matters. I disposed of the damaged articles, cleaned up as much as I could and just got on with it.

Some months passed, and life returned to what passed for normal in my peculiar little world. There was a lot of banging and drilling going on, and builders coming and going, and general pandemonium such as that, but I paid it no heed and remained in my ever moulding chair in front of my clapped out telly, which had, by some trick of fate, survived being saturated. Life sucked, but it was as it should be. Then one day I was wandering around the building when I bumped into the chap who lived down stairs. The very same chap who had suffered so much at my hands. The very man who had glimpsed my vista from Hell shortly after I had moved in, all of ten years previously.

He told me he had claimed on his insurance following the flood, and invited me to take a look. I took a look, and was dumbfounded. His flat had been done up goodo!

Brilliant, I thought, thanked him, and went back to vegetating in my rotten little patch, never once thinking that I might do the same thing. As luck would have it, I met the same kindly gentleman again shortly after that, he pressed a business card into my hand and said "Give this lad a call. You have nothing to lose". Thinking I hadn't got a hope, and it's far too late now anyway, I dialled the number. It was an assessor called Kieran. I told him my flat had been damaged without any real expectation, and he proceeded to go ballistic on the other end of the line. He spoke at ninety miles an hour, and most of it went over my head, but the upshot was, he would take on my case and if I had not called when I did, at the eleventh hour, all hope would have been lost.

So I left it in his hands, and a long and protracted process began, involving him, the insurance company, the management company and a wonderful builder from Galway who ultimately restored my faith in humanity.

To cut a long story short, everything was miraculously agreed, and, while the work got under way, I had the inestimable pleasure of going to stay with my dear sister Neenee and her family in Ennis. I stayed for four months and enjoyed the kindest hospitality ever bestowed upon a man. There is no kinder woman on Earth, her children are angels, and I was truly blessed, but the four months quickly passed, and it was time to head home.

Around the same time, we suddenly started making bonus after bonus at work, right out of the blue, and I received an enormous tax rebate. Suddenly the price of a new telly, bed, suite of furniture, and literally everything else I required, was covered and then some! I purchased all the new stuff and moved in. Words fail me here, but I shall endeavour to impress upon you the sheer magnitude of this event. I found myself in a palace!!

The builder had installed dry wall insulation that made everything as warm as toast for all eternity, and I had wonderful double glazing installed throughout. There was an ultra-modern lighting system straight out of Star Trek, new floors, ceilings, doors, and walls throughout, and I mean everywhere. Not one centimetre of my old shithole remained. It was all gone forever, just a decade long bad dream. The furniture and bed were of the highest standard imaginable, and the coup de grace – new kitchen and bathroom that would not be out of place at an ideal homes exhibition. It was the single most incredible thing that ever happened to me. I had been saved by a man I had previously bombarded with disgusting detritus! Gift upon gift had just fallen into my lap, but this could not have been mere luck. This had to have been directed from behind scenes.

There were unseen hands at work, of this I am sure. Everything fell into place so naturally as to render it unnatural. It was all just too convenient. No man receives a life time of good luck in the space of a few months, and I had previously lived my life under the influence of a malevolent gypsy's curse. Things like that just didn't go my way, and something on this scale was just beyond the parameters of reason. I have a theory about the origins of my god fortune, but like Darwin himself, I fear it may be considered preposterous. It would be ridiculed by right thinking men, and I myself would have scoffed at it before and event in my life convinced me otherwise. It is also something I cannot take lightly. Inclusion in this book at this point may not be wise, as it is something I fear might be reduced to the realms of the facetious if it is.

There is a sacred element, and I am reluctant to talk about it until the time is right, as such a thing must be treated with the utmost respect and without a hint of flippancy. Suffice to say, that I, Sid Sullivan, being of sound mind, and not prone to wild flights of fancy, with my feet firmly rooted in the ground, am certain of the existence of supernatural entities, having had occasion to be visited by one, and that I am also sure in the knowledge that influence is wielded over my life the one that came to me.

The only thing that mankind can be sure of it that mankind cannot be sure of anything, and the only thing I can be sure of is that there is more to mankind than meets the eye. I will tell you in great detail about the experience that brought about this certainty in my mind. The time must be right, however, and believe it or not, I believe I am not supposed to at this point. So ends the writing which was committed to paper by Sid Sullivan on Jan 3rd 2013.

The Tenner

The beauty of writing lies in the fact that possibilities
are endless, and a chap can say just about anything
he pleases. Limitless scope abounds! Rules are there
to be broken and there are no taboos! The thing that
appeals to me most, however, is not the writing, or
the diversity of its content, but the actual physical
act of putting pen to paper. I love to see the nib of a
pen, being controlled by something I am not wholly
certain of, flowing across the surface of a page as it
negotiates its way to the end of that page, which will
be in this case, a moment of great celebration, as
this is page is on the left, and I fear they have to
invent a new phobia for me, as I have a quare sort of
aversion to writing on the left, and would much
prefer to write on the right, as is my right, as a
writer, right?

Forgive my scandalous assumption, I know I do not
qualify as a writer just because I allow the nib of a
pen to tune into a weakly flowing stream of
consciousness, but I am not playing volleyball here.
It is the physical act of writing, even if the results
cannot be described as such. Furthermore, I intend
to continue, and I shall cast a blind eye over any
particularly glaring literary blunders, as it is my right

as a volleyball player to screw up as much as I please.

Is it a book? Is it a journal? Is it a diary? Just what the bleeding hell is it?

Well, right now it is just a beautiful virgin right sided page for which I am very grateful, for it is Saturday morning, I am having a bottle of orange and taking up space at a well-known fast food joint. If I appear to be prevaricating, I do apologise, and I have to admit that I have yet to stumble upon a topic of conversation. Pause, while I sup some orange.

It it a manuscript? Just a script? A memoir? A monumentally melancholy missal, or just a repository for aimless alliteration? I am not sure, if the truth be told, but I am sure it will fulfil many roles, like the ones mentioned, and perhaps some more, that we possibly cannot think of right now, or at a stretch, some that have yet to be invented.

Books, for instance, have been known to come in handy when carrying out the act of euthanasia on budgerigars, but thankfully we will not be reduced to that, as we have to establish whether or not this is a book.

There is something about my bench at work. It is the most accommodating and comfortable work space imaginable. Creative juices just flow like irrepressible torrents as I sit there. It seems a terrible shame to me. I am required to produce work for a company while I am there, and not work for myself. I can't imagine how much art could have sprung from these hands over the past 21 years, had I been allowed to create whatever I pleased.

My mind, due to my age, is becoming mercifully uncluttered, and I am far more at ease with myself, but an unfortunate consequence of having my head free from distracting complications is the empty vessel that no masquerades as my mind. But never mind, I don't need a fully functioning intellect anymore. Such a thing would serve no purpose. In order to complete this book, what's left of my mind must be mined. We must delve into the banks of experience, we must attempt to illuminate the places, persons and events that took place in my inconsequential life, and in doing so, attempt to produce something of reasonable consequence.

I am approaching fifty years of age. I must have blinked, for a large part of my life has vanished in an instant, and if I blink again I shall end up six foot under. So perhaps it is an appropriate time to pen some form of memoir.

Reaching this age is nothing short of remarkable, not least since I have felt myself to be on the verge of expiration since I was just a slip of a lad, but also because it affords a chap a chance to distance himself from his past. It is very much like surveying a story from a lofty perch. Although that was my life, I now feel quite separated from it, but most importantly, I am able to decipher the good from the bad, I can now really appreciate the wonders that my way and enjoy a profound sense of gratitude for things that I did not fully appreciate at the time.

I can also cast a cold, calculating eye over all the despicable things I did and treat the perpetrator of these crimes as he imposter that he surely is, safe in the knowledge that my path in future has been formed by a great guiding hand, and it shall be littered with nothing but acts of selfless compassion.

There is an event from my youth that occupies the realm of über important. It shaped my destiny from the point of its occurrence, and can be considered a major turning point. I shall attempt to relate it to you, but please ensure that you are sitting comfortably, for it is a very long story.

A vast part of my school days were spent playing truant with my dear friend Brendan Coyne. With the help of his big brother, and my big sister's future husband, we constructed a supremely marvellous fort in the forest of Tullyglass Hill, which overlooked our various abodes. We would spend our days in the magnificent construction, subsisting on milk pilfered from local doorsteps and Mars bars illegally liberated from the local supermarket, Maurice Platt's emporium, Quinsworth.

At the start of Third Year at our beloved comprehensive school, however, our absence for the entire previous term was noted, the local builders repatriated their manifold materials, deconstructed our sacred sanctuary, and our mitching days came to an end. It was time to face the dreaded intermediate certification, and we had to go to school.

In those days however, wild horses could not drag me from my slumber. Sleep would overtake me completely, and although it could be temporarily disrupted with a sharp slap or a bucket of cold water, it would be resumed in a blissful instant. My long suffering mother had my forced awakening foisted upon her on a daily basis and it has to be said that the incomparable Patty Brennan was the only person on this Earth capable of doing so. I shall not elaborate on the methods she employed, to spare readers of a sensitive disposition, but it did compel me to name the procedures at the time. I christened them – "The Early Morning Jabberwocks" and I am grateful that middle age has now rendered them unnecessary.

I was highly susceptible to the love bug back in those heady days, and my mind was very much on my latest obsession as I fitfully fretted in my unkempt scratcher the night before the big day, and a combination of the Jaberwocks and the idea of laying my eyes on her again this day were enough to propel me toward my destination. So I moseyed along, in an unhurried fashion, for a chap cannot hurry these things. A sense of dread overtook me as I neared my date with academia.

Ghastly visions of terrifying ghouls plagued me, for in my adolescent estimation, school was an institution populated by cruel demons. Everyday appeared to be an eternity as I stared forlornly out into the fields and freedom, and the fact that I was in love with every girl there resident, made learning impossible, as erotic distractions abounded. But there was only one girl on my mind as I trudged slowly along the road that fateful morning. A coquettish young dream, fluffy and whimsical in her demeanour, sly and mysterious, her brown eyes had me entranced. Her manifold charms all wrapped up in an enigmatic entity that inhabited my every waking thought, and although like me, she was a mere sixteen years old, in my eyes she was a true woman of the world, and if the world was aware of her like I was, she would have been placed on a pedestal for all mankind to worship at her feet.

My heart ached with unrequited adoration as I meandered along the gloomy morning street, my head bowed in morose resignation. Just then, with a mere two hundred yards left of my journey, I made a discovery that considerably brightened my day. On the grass verge, for all the world to see, lay a shiny, crisp and uncreased ten pound note. The answer to my dreams, for in 1980, ten pounds constituted a fortune.

I was suddenly a rich kid. I thought to myself, "I shall no longer merely be Sid the Kid, from this day on I shall be Sid the rich Kid," and I did a jig of delight as I quickly pocketed my prize.

"Where were you last year?" my form teacher asked, as I took my seat on that first day back. "Mitching, sir" I replied, to rampant general hilarity. I was an instant hero to my peers, and a very rich one at that. I revelled in my new found fame for a period, as I plotted to sell ice cubes to Arabs and achieve ultimate world domination.

My reverie, however, was suddenly interrupted by the familiar crackle of the school intercom system and the dreaded voice of the 'boss'. "Amaleascail, amaleascail" he opined. (I believe this is Gaelic for "attention please", though I can't be sure.) "A sum of money has been lost, could the finder please hand it into the office, thank you" and the public address system whirred and crackled to a sudden stop as my heartbeat increased incrementally. "Shit" I thought, and began to deliberate on my sudden dilemma. After some time I concluded that the money in all likelihood belongs to one of those horrible greasy Mods. A shower of shysters that constantly bombard us Freaky Dudes with snotty projectiles. If I keep the money, it will be a kind of revenge against them, and the decision was made. To hell with the Mods, I was rich, and I was staying that way!

I met my fellow Freaky Dudes at eleven. We shared a single cigarette, and got quite bombed in the process, without of course, letting on to each other. I blurted out, in a slurred sort of fashion, my incredible news. "I found a tenner lads! I'm rich!" I gleefully imparted, and needless to say, my announcement was greeted with great excitement. A mini parliament was suddenly assembled, and the question of the tenner, and what we are going to do with it, was discussed in great detail. Should it be a bottle of whiskey and twenty Goldbond each, or a bottle of vodka and twenty Rothmans each? Was the question, and before the bell went to signal the end of break, we had decided upon the latter option and returned to class, to stare, no doubt, at our respective unobtainable infatuations.

After school, we assembled down the shops. Or the shop, as it was in Shannon in those days. We waited for assistance, until it came in the shape of an amenable eighteen year old, who promptly purchased a large bottle of vodka on our behalf, in return for the price of ten fags. (Ten quid certainly stretched back then, and no mistake!) With our canine companions, Bruce, yogi, Scotty and Fred in tow, we headed to the local barber shop, a small operation that went by the name of "Henderson's Hairlines" and were granted entry by our friend, an apprentice barber whose boss was on holiday. He put up the 'closed' sign, we sat in the hairdressing chairs, fun things of the swivelling variety, lit up the smokes and passed the bottle between us.

Now vodka, as you may know, is a very deceptive drink. Drunkenness does not always immediately register, and I sat in my swivel chair until the bottle was drained, quite under the impression that I was sober as a judge. The lads had started dying each other's hair and were up to all sorts of shenanigans as I got up to go outside. I opened the door, and saw one of our dear doggies, Yogi, sitting on the path. "Aw, Yogi." I said, and staggered toward him. The air outside had suddenly caused sever inebriation to inhabit my young personage, and as I bent down to pet Yogi, I just kept right on going. And going. I hit the kerb with my two front teeth, knocking them clean out, and lay there in a stupefied heap as the barber party raged on. My lunch came through the gap where my teeth used to be as I began to vomit in bucketloads. I must have been a right puke covered toothless spectacle as I staggered, gibbering, towards home.I was only vaguely aware that my teeth were gone as I climbed in the back window of our house on the hill and collapsed into bed, still vomiting profusely as the drink sent me into a coma.

When the early morning Jabberwocks showed up next morning, they were greeted with quite a sight. There in bed, was Patty Brennan's former son. Now a gummy old man, his matted hair caked with diced carrots and other unidentifiable food stuffs. As he lay there in abject terror, the realisation of the previous day's events slowly dawning on him. He opened his mouth, gurgled incoherently, and his poor mother fainted on the spot. But she was soon to recover her senses and the wailing and gnashing of teeth began in earnest. She was lucky, she still had teeth, the apparition before her was just beginning to realise that two of his most crucial gnashers were no more. "G'shmorning, Mammy" I weakly uttered, and I knew I would have to come up with a reason for this shambles, and pronto. My young brain went into hyper-overdrive as my mom retreated to the kitchen in a state of dumbfounded bewilderment. I showered and cleaned up as best I could, like a good little lad, putting on my angelic side as I went to join her.

"It wasn't my fault, mom" I began, with my best look of injured innocence. "I was just walking home yesterday when I was attacked by a gang of vicious boot-boys! Honest to God, they pushed a bottle of vodka into my mouth and knocked out my teeth! They forced me to drink the whole bottle! I don't remember what happened after that!" And so the bullshit flowed, and to this day, I don't know if my mum fell for it, but I think she wanted to believe it, and It may have just been preposterous enough to be plausible.

My appointment with the tooth doctor was hastily arranged, and I attended forthwith. After many agonising hours, and numerous dates with dentistry, much to my dismay, I was fitted with a ghastly denture. A horrible, slimy, pink thing with two goofy teeth attached. It was just a temporary measure, until my gums receded enough to perform the real work. Meantime, the bills were mounting, and my folks informed me that it was my responsibility to pay.

As it happened, the previous year's mitching off school, coupled with the permanent state of romantic distraction that I was in, was beginning to take its toll on my school work, and I began to fall slightly behind the others, and to top it all, I had an attitude. I didn't need school. I didn't fit in. I had a problem with authority. After many a pow wow with my folks, a plan was formulated. I would do the inter-cert, which was now imminent, leave school, get a job, and pay the dentist bills.

Around this time news began to filter though as to the rightful owner of that infamous ten pound note. You guessed it, it was the girl of my dreams. She had lost her book money at the start of term, and her family being not so well off, and a bit stricken with poverty, she was forced to share books with others until she could replace the tenner. I was crushed, and could never look into those big brown eyes again. Had I given her the tenner, like I should have, who knows what might have happened. Greed got the better of me, and due to my selfish actions, I now found myself propelled into the big bad world of job seeking.

Adulthood had been thrust upon me, and my days of innocence were over. The dentist turned out to be a genius, and he fixed me up good and proper with some excellent bridge work. I still see him to this day, 33 years later, and he has not changed a bit, leading me to believe that he is in fact a dental robot, manufactured to the highest standards somewhere in Japan. I have an appointment with him very soon in fact. I am almost looking forward to it.

Honesty is always the best policy, as this story demonstrates, but things also happen for a reason. I was soon to find a job, the greatest job I could have landed, I was to become a layout artist in the local printers! Oh joy of joys! I was to be a working artist! So at the tender age of seventeen, I began, and it was indeed wonderful. For almost a year I beavered away, producing posters and pamphlets, and even designing logos for local companies. I was however, still on seventeen, I still had an attitude, and crucially, I had yet to master the art of getting out of bed! The job was short lived, but I am left with marvellous memories. It was the start of my working life, and I could have asked for better.

So ends this story. The effects of those events so long ago till reverberate, of course, and always shall. I would like to say that I learned many valuable lessons from the experience, but it was really just the beginning of my wanton ways and I was to be a somewhat corrupt individual for most of my days thereafter.

1976

In 1976, long before the ten pound note and my
dramatic change of direction, the family resided a
while in Dublin. My mother is a Dublin girl through
and through, and never really took to life among the
refugees in Shannon. So she convinced my dear old
dad to move the whole operation to Artane. My dad
acquired a flat, and commuted up and down the
ancient highways and byways of Ireland.

I was twelve, and leaving Shannon was a wrench,
but it was out of my hands and off we went. We
waved goodbye to the town I loved so well and
headed for the darkest abyss I shall ever experience.
Dublin in all its dreary drudgery is no place for a
greenhorn little English boy who only really knew life
in Shannon, an ideal playground for any kid, and
little did I know, things were about to go from bad to
worse.

My experience of school in Shannon, and before that
in Sussex, had been perfectly delightful. Developing
childhood rushes on girls and enjoying myself
immensely, while the teachers were always nothing
short of super. I was subjected to the softly softly
approach to education, and it was all I knew. I had
been successfully moulded into a well-adjusted little

chap who had not a care in the world! But I had a soft underbelly, and was ill prepared for the next level of my education.

"I have found you a school" were to prove to be the most disturbing words ever to emanate from my mother's mouth. "It's six miles away, in Donnycarney, but we'll find it." She said, as we set off on a bleak winter morning, walking as my dad had the car down in good old Shannon town.

After what seemed like a trek across the Himalayas on the back of a tortoise, we finally came across St. Chiaráin's Christian Brother School, Donnycarney, in the county of Dublin. "They're expecting you", said the Ma, and I took my first tentative steps into Hell. I entered a huge gloomy hall, replete with cobwebs and dim sunlight that struggled to escape from partially drawn blinds.

The darkness was the first thing to hit me, a second later, a Christian Brother was the second thing to hit me. I thought he was some description of a friendly monk or something benign such as that as he approached, but appearances can be deceptive, and this colossal gargoyle in a skirt reached out and clattered me a right wallop before demanding "What in the name of Jesus and all the saints are you doing here, boy!?" I began to blubber a little, and he smiled. "Ah. You must be the new boy, follow me" and I reluctantly complied. We went to his office, for as it turned out, he was the head honcho.

After taking my name, we enjoyed a little chit-chat. "So, what do you like to do, Mr O'Sullivan?" he enquired. "Er... I like footy and cricket, and I support Man United" I replied. At this, his brotherliness seemed to suddenly vanish, and he went purple with rage.

"That's a very English accent you have there, boy! But not to worry! We'll soon have it banished!" he bawled. He grabbed me by the collar and shoved me up against the wall. "Hands out straight! Palms up!" he shrieked, as he produced from his drawer something I had never seen before, but something I was to become very much acquainted with. An instrument of indescribable torture. The leather! The leather was a device designed to inflict maximum agony to the hand, buttock, inner thigh and other sensitive areas belonging to children unfortunate enough to come into contact with it. It was around ten inches long and three inches thick and came complete with a handle.

Beelzebub and his minions were employed somewhere in the depths of Hell itself to manufacture these outrageous instruments of

torture. As I found out on that first day of jolly old
St. Chiaráin's, one slap from this repugnant strap
would leave a kid floundering in feverish anguish for
hours. The pain was so intense, so altogether
shocking, so beyond endurance that it would literally
leave a chap traumatised for a month afterwards.
"That will drive the Sasanach scum out of ya!" did
scream our supreme master as he took his revenge
for 800 years of British oppression out on me.

He left me sitting for at least an hour after my first
leathering, in his office. While he went in search of
fresh victims, I'm sure, and upon his return, he was
all smiles again. "Right, English!" he beamed, for that
now appeared to be my name, "Get up the stairs, go
to room ten, that will be your class from now on. And
don't let me see you down here again!"

So off I went to room ten, and fresh horrors. The
teacher, a layman by the name of Mr Hoey, asked me
to introduce myself to the class, to whom it was
obvious that I'd just spent the last hour in complete
shock and bawling my eyes out. "Er... I'm Kevin... I
like cricket..." Yes indeed, I played right into their
hands as the assembled boys guffawed with laughter
and cries of "He's a fuckin' English eejit" rose above
the thick chalk dust.

A hard element, my new classmates. Street urchins from the unforgiving back roads of North Dublin in the seventies. Hard as nails, they were, to a man. There were no girls either, it was just us men, and Mr Hoey, the master.

Morning break arrived, and we were herded en masse into a high walled exercise yard. I didn't know anyone, so I stood by the bicycle shed, alone, idly tapping the wall with my toe to pass the time. Before I knew it, I was unceremoniously manhandled by some black clad monster back into the master of masters' office, where I was to be leathered again. My crime? Lifting my foot in the yard.

An indoctrination that is as fresh in memory now as it was then, and the following year would be just as unforgettable for all the wrong reasons.

I was a disoriented mess after that first day, and it took hours to find my way home, my sense of direction never having been that sharp. My mother was frantic, and when I fell into the house blubbering my little brains out, raving about monsters and pleading with her not to send me back, she was more than a little taken aback, but regretfully for me, she remained steadfastly uncompromising. "You have to go to school. We all had to go through it. Stand up and be a man."

Our neighbour, Mr Kennedy, had offered to bring me
to school in his car, as he was dropping off his
daughter, the delectable Geraldine, at the girl's
school up the road. I can still see her in that pretty
little uniform as the theme to my torment played on
the radio. Every morning, at the same time 'Don't
Cry for Me Argentina' played as we set out from
Artane into the fires of Hades.

It was a huge hit, and remained at number one for a
considerable time. It was the perfect mournful
lament and I came to associate it with my impending
doom.

Every morning praying that something would deliver
me from being delivered to those gates. Anything. A
crash. An earthquake. Anything! Shut up, Julie
Covington! What have you got to cry about anyway?
A typical day would start with the master to see our
homework, which we called 'ecker'. He would then
peruse it for a brief time as the class sat in silence.
Then the rest of the day was given over to
leatherings, with a half hour period at the end given
over to leathering a lad called Emmet, coz he
absolutely never, ever, did his ecker!

We were leathered if we could not point out an Irish
county on the map, if we could not recite our times
tables, and if our writing went over the margin in our

copy book. Never mind if we got everything right, because everybody had to have their daily leathering, with extra helpings for Emmet.

I literally used to pray at night that Emmet would do his bloody homework! The last two hours of a Friday were given over to 'games'. Hordes of little hard nuts would be let loose in the field to kick seven shades of shit out of one and another. I remember my first session. "Can ya foight, English?" I was asked. When I replied that I preferred to play cricket, I was smothered by masses of these little gurriers, who proceeded to beat me black and blue. But I soon learned to fight, and I gained their respect after a time.

Corporal punishment, I believe, was banned in Irish schools a few years later, and those persecutory pillocks, the brothers, hardly exist anymore. There are a few grizzled old geezers waiting for their imminent final judgement scattered about, but the brothers, effectively, are no more. We do of course, still have the memories. It was like inhabiting a particularly grim Charles Dickens novel, without the proverbial moralistic ending, for there were no morals, and there was no ending. Just dat day after day of relentless terror.

I got off lightly, as I think the master took a bit of a shine to me. He once leathered a little chap called Mannix half to death, because he had the temerity to beat me in a game of chess. According to the master, Mannix had threatened me with personal injury if I won. He did, but he was only messing, and he beat me fair and square. I had to sit and watch as poor Mannix was viciously assaulted, knowing full well that he was an innocent man.

I didn't know where the Irish counties could be located on the map when I started, but by the end I was an expert on the geography of Hibernia. We had the heroism of Irish rebels constantly drilled into us and I soon became well educated on that subject too. Robert Emmet, Wolfe Tone, Michael Collins and streams of other martyrs to the cause soon became very familiar to me, and I suddenly developed great diligence in my application to my studies.

I would still get my daily leathering as Mr Hoey didn't want to exclude me from the fun, but didn't hit me as often or as hard as some of those other poor little devils.

I often wonder what became of my classmates, a more decent collection of little thugs never existed, and we were all in it together, to a man.

Life in Artane wasn't all bad, and during the holidays it was perfectly agreeable. Up until August of '77, I had really begun to enjoy myself. My pal Ray would call around every morning without fail, and we would spend endless hours kicking a ball about in the field adjacent to our house. I developed a liking for his sister, Sandra, and life regained its sense of perspective. It was all about football and girls again, and I began to settle in dear old Dublin at long last. Times and dates are now a little jumbled up in my memory, but I believe it as in August 1977 that my dad had his first heart attack. With apologies to you, Dad, if I am mixing you up with Elvis Presley.

One day, while commuting, my dad had his first attack, but luckily my big sister was with him in the car. She flagged down a truck, and Pop survived. That however, was the end of our time in Dublin, and before I knew it, I was sitting on the boiler with Pascal.

I remember discussing the demise of Elvis with him, so I can safely say that it was August 1977. Scandalously, we had no regard for The King, and to us, he was just an aging Lothario in a jumpsuit. Most importantly, I was back in Shannon, and the most marvellous of times got underway. 1978 was just around the corner, the most memorable of years, but this time, for all the right reasons.

Secondary School began, and I was enrolled in St. Patrick's Comprehensive. A very typical educational institution for a small provincial town, but a very special place if you are a fourteen year old on your first day there.

A whole new world opened up to me, there was no physical punishment employed, although some of the incumbent educators attempted to appear threatening with various degrees of success. And most crucially, it was a uni-sex establishment!

I became acquainted with folk who would become life-long friends, extraordinary characters one and all. We were just snot-nosed juveniles, but attending this school, in our eyes, somehow bestowed a super cool sophistication upon us. My attendance was good in first year and I found a kind of niche in English class.

We had a brilliant teacher, the best I ever had, and she brought the best out of me. She would read my essays to the class. They were very well received, and I enjoyed many a proud moment. She put on a production of the Brendan Behan play 'The New House' with yours truly starring as Shaybo Hannigan. We put on many performances and won many awards. Life was good, until I came upon the young woman who was soon to become my first real infatuation.

I became totally besotted with her, literally adoring the ground she walked on. In my young eyes, ours was a great love affair, on a par with Heathcliffe and Cathy, and in hers, it was just a passing tryst.

It was heartbreak, and it was my first experience of it. I would camp outside her house, hoping for a glimpse of her feminine features. If she so much as looked at me, I would come over all faint, and if she spoke to me, even just to say "Piss off and leave me alone" I would dine out for a week. I once paid a huge sum in order to purchase an LP record because the girl on the cover bore a faint resemblance to her. I would sit and cry over her constantly. I loved her. It was all consuming, and totally and utterly ridiculous.

I eventually recovered my senses, but it set a trend, and I continued to fall deeply in love with unobtainable females at the drop of a hat.

It was in June of '78 when I had this initial dalliance with my first love. Just one of the elements that contributed to the perfect summer.

It was really the last of the innocent times, with the onset of the age of sex, drugs and rock'n'roll just around the corner. Little did we know, but as we sat in awestruck wonderment, beholding that gargantuan celestial fireball, our childhood was drawing to a close, and the first signs of adult cynicism entered our adolescent psyche.

Intermission

My pen has developed a momentum all of its own in
recent days and to be honest, I have been struggling
to keep up with it. I must reign it in, and re-enter the
present.

Indeed, the present would be a good place to start,
before my trusty black bic insists on taking us off on
a mystery tour yet again. Wherever shall it take us
next?

This little writing exercise is starting to take on
proportions that I never expected. If I'd known I was
going to be writing a book I might have given some
thought to its content. I tell myself that I have taken
a giant leap forward in attempting to create a
complete manuscript that has no reliance on
structure or logic, but then I remember, James Joyce
got there before me.

I am struggling to define exactly what I am doing
here, and the longer the write the more convinced I
become that my frivolous attitude toward the English
language, so far I think, displayed in abundance, is
ultimately going to lead me, and you, into oblivion.
Next stop: oblivion.

Unlike my good self in my youth, my grasp of the
language is now hopelessly inadequate. Or is it just

that I had youth on my side then, and could get away with such glaring foibles? I shall continue, unabated, safe in the knowledge that my grammer, my spelling, and the structure of my sentences, in the grand scheme of things, doesn't matter a damn. I am currently coming to you from my comfy chair at home. It is early on a Wednesday morning and I am enjoying the silver lining that comes with a heavy cold, namely, a day off. It is my second one in a row, and though I have been going stir crazy, I am grateful to have such a well-appointed venue in which to go around the bend.

Recent bulletins seem to indicate that I am indeed trying to pen some form of memoir here, purely by accident, I assure you, as I had no idea what I was doing when I set out. Staff members at work are given these lovely diaries on an annual basis, and for the past 21 years I have looked on, consumed with resentment and jealousy. I mean to say! They don't even write anything in them! They keep them in their desk drawers, occasionally jotting some inconsequential note or other until they are half filled with trivial tripe, and then they are given brand spanking new one!

But I wasn't having it this year, and I was in luck, as an old friend of mine had recently started in reception, and when the diaries became available, I chanced my arm and went to see her, cap in hand. She is a delightful woman, and was most kind. She furnished me with this book, and I would just like to apologise publicly to her at this point, for I once compared her to a rather buxom Australian soap opera character.

It was in one of my long lost early diaries, and 'Beany' as she is affectionately known, was most dismayed to read it. If you are reading this, Beany, rest assured, for you do not bear the slightest resemblance to Shirley from 'A Country Practice' and do, in fact, stand quite alone. You are beyond compare!

I thank you sincerely for giving me this thought depository, because I know you took a risk in doing so and it isn't quite the done thing, shall we say. Without it, I would not be able to compile my accidental memoirs, which reminds me, shouldn't I e doing that right now?

But where do I start?

At the beginning, you say?

Alright. I will point the car in the direction of the coffee shop, purchase myself a hot liquid stimulant, and attempt to do just that.

Gargle! Slurp! Gargle!

Ah.

That's better, biro amphetamines!

Here we go! Hold onto your hats!

Childhood

I have vague memories of having my nappies changed. I undertook an experiment once, recommended to me by some obscure professor on a daytime TV show. It involved lying on your bed and bringing your feet up behind your ears. I must have done this many years ago, as it would no doubt cause me great injury if I tried it now. I won't go into any further gruesome details, but it does indeed bring all sorts of memories flooding back and a very familiar feeling overtakes a chap.

If you fancy having a go, be sure that you are alone in the house, and fully clothed.

My first post-nappy memory is of the Rolling Stones. I believe I may have been one and a bit years old. The Rolling Stones were gyrating around inside our prehistoric TV set, making a noise that was indistinguishable to my barely formed ears, but one of the adults present started dancing around the room, and another one said something akin to "That's the Rolling Stones!"

In this, a picture formed in my baby mind that I can still recall in perfect clarity. I must have been familiar with stones, perhaps having played with them in the garden, and I somehow grasped the concept of the same stones in the act of rolling, in this case down a hill. Nothing gives me greater 'Satisfaction' than to be able to relate this story to you, because the Stones are the bee's knees in my estimation. It is nothing short of incredible, but they are still rolling, and have formed the soundtrack to my entire life.

In my humble opinion, 'Jumping Jack Flash' is the single most magnificent work of art ever created, but more about that great ban anon, I hope, and back to what I can remember from the 1960s. Hey man! I was there!

In 1968, when I was four, I became aware of a man who was to become my childhood here. It was the European Cup final and George Best lit up our little screen as I jumped around the front room in a frenzy. I was football mad, and I had just seen a real wizard in action.

(I say that with a sense of irony, because I am writing in a coffee shop, but we won't dwell on it.)

George Best was not of this Earth. There are modern day footballers that are deservedly feted, but none could hold a candle to him. He wasn't just brilliant, he was cool, and I think perhaps my four year old self had designs on one day being just as cool, because even then, I knew, I would never be able to

59

dribble like that, even if I did completely inhabit this soccer behemoth, becoming Georgie every time I donned y beloved United kit (fashioned from red curtains and socks with stripes sewn into them.)

He provided my happiest childhood memories, a lot of which involve standing outside TV shops on Saturday mornings hoping to glimpse him on one of the screens, and some of my frustrating, as right up to my mid-teens he kept screwing up, and I despaired so much for him.

It doesn't happen often, but his eventual, inevitable, untimely death reduced me to a blubbering mess of tears, and I still balk at the injustice of it all.

I spent the rest of the sixties clowning about in Pound Hill, Crawley, Sussex and attending my first school, which was called Our Lady Queen of Heaven. I loved that school. I had a mate called Terence Corrigan, my first best pal, and I was vaguely aware of the fact that I enjoyed being in the company of two girls form my class. Clare Barklett and Yvonne Hardy. How early it begins!

I remember creating a snake charmer out of plasticine, and being sent to show it to the headmistress, a kindly old nun called Sister Mary-John. She cooed with delight, and I was aware for the first time that I might be an artist.

The seventies came along, and decimalisation was a big deal. I remember that distinctly, because I would no longer get sixpence a week pocket money. I got ten new pence instead, and you could get as many sweets with that! I had yet to learn to read, but I was obsessed with comics, notably 'Buster' which included my favourite character, a young fellow called FACEACHE who could "scrounge" his features into the most fabulous disfigurations.

My weeks were also not complete without 'Roy of the Rovers' and I was altogether convinced that the goings on in that comic were totally real. It was a comic book world of ghastly distorted mugs and unfeasible last minute hat-tricks.

I was an innocent little English boy in short trousers, plimsolls and knee-length grey socks.

In Crawley, as I have mentioned, we lived on the grass verge of Tilgate Forest, where I served my Junior Tarzan of the Jungle apprenticeship. I was a proper little wild boy of Borneo for a spell. It instilled in me a great love of nature, and to this day, I will occasionally stare out the window at it. (Nature that is; I need to get out more.)

I graduated from infant school with snake charmer honours, and entered the real thing, a huge, rambling and ancient establishment called St.

Francis of Assisi Catholic School. I used to sit on a bench outside the gates, waiting to be picked up, with a wee girl called Claire. We became firm friends, in as much as it's possible for children of such a tender age to do so.

I can see her in my mind's eye as I write this, swinging her little feet under the bench and smiling at me.

Then one day, I sat at the bench alone, wondering where she was. My lift arrived, I got in, and asked my mom. "Where's Claire?"

"She won't be there anymore" she said softly, and went on to explain that on the previous day, after Claire had been picked up by her folks, they had stopped at a garage to get petrol. She somehow contrived to open the back door of their estate car, and fell out just as they were reversing away. They ran her over, but she seemed unharmed. They put her back in the car, and started towards the hospital. The poor mite died a few minutes later.

It was my first experience of the transient nature of life and of course, death itself. I could not take it in, and kept picturing this terrible event in my mind, convinced that I could still intervene and make everything alright.

To make matters worse, Gilbert O'Sullivan was enjoying a massive hit with his song 'Claire' at the time, and I was sure he was singing about my little friend.

May she rest in peace, little Claire, just a child, denied a chance at life.

Memories of my English childhood are a vague, jumbled up, collection of snippets now. Predominantly, they involve looking out of car windows at the Sussex countryside whizzing by. I remember being in just such a car with my two kid sisters on one occasion. It was being driven by a very sweet old dear with blue hair and lasses perched on the end of her nose.

She was going to a country fete, but was to drop the three of us home first. In the back of the car, just behind us, was a huge box. It had a hole in the top, and was decorated in a beautiful fashion by dear old driver. "That's my lucky dip box" she told us, "You won't touch it, will you?"

I still try to picture the scene at that fete, as paying customers dip their hands into the old lady's box, rummage around, and find absolutely nothing. We were holy little terrors, and no mistake.

In those days, no matter what I was doing, I would somehow manage to be standing at the garden gate at five o'clock, on a daily basis, come rain, hail, or whatever you're having yourself.

I would call off the little footy match, climb down from the tree, or emerge from the mucky bomb crater every say at the same time. It was imperative, you see, that I meet my dad as soon as he came home from work. I would stand there in anxious anticipation awaiting the big moment, and sure enough, he never let me down. He would saunter toward me, a spring in his step and a smile on his face, he would tap the top of my head with his newspaper and always say exactly the same thing. Tow little words that seemed to validate my entire existence. "Good man" he would say, and it would instil within me an inner glow that seemed to make sense of everything.

I would then resume my activities with renewed enthusiasm until I was dragged in for tea, pyjamas, and bed. I never had trouble sleeping, because I was a "good man" and God himself was smiling benignly at me from his lofty perch in the clouds.

Two magic words, Dad, and I will never be able to thank you enough.

I am no longer resident in the coffee shop, in fact, I am coming to you live from my doctor's waiting room. I have been attending the same doctor since my early teens, and like my dentist, he has changed not one single iota. Something peculiar is going on in the medical profession. Methinks they may have discovered the immortality serum and are keeping it to themselves.

As ever, the waiting room is populated by attractive young mothers. I was doing well to begin with, and they may or may not have been intrigued by the bloke writing in the book, but I have just spoiled the moment by sneezing my arse off, quickly followed by a passable impression of a foghorn.

I seek a sick note, I shall procure it from my trusty GP and beat a hasty retreat. The swimming pool beckons. Possibly not the best treatment for flu-like symptoms, but I can always be trusted to do things in an unconventional fashion. In this regard, consistency is my middle name.

Splish! Splash! Mission accomplished.

I am still torn between my memoirs a a diary, and have become terrified of boring any potential readers to death with either, so I have left it up to my biro to decide what to do. It is touching the page with its nib and moving around in an apparently arbitrary manner.

But something ensues, it seems, so let's go with it. And interesting side effect of big bugs such as the one that has afflicted me all week, is the resulting anaesthesia. I haven't felt a thing since Monday, and it now being Thursday, a multitude of bodily appendages might have separated themselves from my person, and I wouldn't even have noticed.

I noticed when I came out of the pool today that a huge chunk of skin was hanging off my index finger. Right where the pen makes an indentation during the act of writing. It seems that this very act of writing has caused some physical damage.

I think they call that suffering for one's art, but I can't be sure, because I can't feel a thing. (And I am not sure if this is art.)

As for trying to dredge up suitable memories from my English childhood, forget it. There is nothing happening. Indeed, it seems I must have spent those years wrapped up in cotton wool, for when I attempt to access the relevant memory banks, cotton wool is all I am met with. Shall we move on, Mr Biro?

We can always return to Crawley Sussex in the 70s at a later date.

Agreed? Ok. Thank you.

Tina

In 1974, we waved bye-bye to dear old Blighty and
Mom, Dad, and their five offspring assembled on the
deck of a car ferry called The Munster, in preparation
for the repatriation of the O'Sullivan clan.

I remember it well, because I was sure there was a
giant spelling mistake on the side of the ship, and it
should have been called 'The Monster'. Funnily
enough though, it was named after the province in
Ireland we were headed for, and in time, we arrived
there safe and sound. The Irish adventure had
begun, and the little English boy in the short pants
was left behind forever.

We must have encountered a lot more cotton wool at
this stage, because that is all I can see as this biro
jumps about in front of me, but we shall persevere.
The other day, when heading to this coffee shop in
which I am now resident again, I was in the process
of walking to my car when I bumped into a very
special lady. Back in 1974, as we were arriving
outside our new home in Shannon, my eyes alighted
upon this very same lady. She was eight or nine, I
suppose, and she had a fleece of shiny red hair
cascading across her little figure.

She herself casts doubts upon my assumption that she was the first person I became aware of in Ireland, but I'm sticking to my story. She became a crucial component in our childhood, befriending me and my sisters, and remains close to us to this day. We had a nice chat, which is always an inestimable privilege. She was the first person I spoke to in Shannon, and funny enough, she was the last, because I haven't spoken to a soul since[*]. I have become the solitary bloke who sits in the corner of a coffee shop pouring his heart out into some mysterious vessel.

Tina, I know you shy away from publicity, but my pen just mentioned your name and it was entirely out of my hands.

Information has just filtered through the cotton wool. Apparently, I have spoken to some people since I met the bold Christina. I spoke to the doctor, and told him I had just included him in this book, which I referred to as my memoirs, and he was very pleased. I also spoke to a number of folks down in the swimming pool.

Parties of school children, who make the shrillest, loudest, and most obnoxious racket known to man, had invaded every available space in the water, forcing me to flee to the steam room. I was vaguely

---

[*] I met her the other day.

aware of another presence in there, and after a long awkward silence, I piped up with the immortal words – "Not much room in here, is there?" To which, a female voice responded by going into paroxysms of laughter. I didn't mean to be amusing, but was chuffed anyway.

We discussed the vagaries of the pool timetable, and got on quite well, although I never did see her face. Oh well. Ships in the night, and all that.

4b Cronan Lawn, was our first address here in Shannon, and we lived there for a couple of years before I went to meet the brothers. They were fascinating times for a kid. Only having been used to other little English kids like myself, it was totally mind expanding, for as it happened, our little town was a refuge for the politically persecuted. It was a heady mix of Chileans and folk from Northern Ireland, with other nationalities added for seasoning. 'Wee girls' would pelt us from their garden at the end of the block, firing projectiles and chanting "Brits out! Brits out!" and it gave us quite a shock at first, but we were soon to ingratiate ourselves and become part of the general community. Kids imitated the prejudices at large in society, and it made no sense, but we gave as good as we got.

The fact that the neighbourhood resembled a cross between the Falls Road and downtown Santiago on a bad day, however, didn't go down very well with my poor mom, and she had a lot of trouble fitting in.

It was easy for us kids, we were just having a laugh, but the ma just couldn't settle. So it turned out that most of my initial friendships were forged with Northern Irish folk, and Chileans that had developed Northern Irish accents. I was truly blessed.

These people possessed all the best qualities humanity had to offer. Loyalty, an enormous spirit born of hardship, and a bottomless well of side-splitting humour.

We had a mad dog named Tarzan who used to eat giant boulders and we revelled in the most amazing sense of freedom ever bestowed upon children.

Myself and my refugee friends did cast off our shackles to live every fantastic day like it was a lifetime. It was so unlike England where children play in designated areas, this town was ours to explore at will.

Life, love, and liberty, by Jupiter, it was an ideal time to be alive. Elvis was still singing and unbridled joy was the order of the day. I thank my lucky stars for the day I first laid eyes on Tina's flaming red mane.

I attended St. Connaire's School in the heart of Cronan, and had many a marvellous experience. The teachers were wonderful. A Miss Hoolahan, and a Mr Brennan in particular.

Miss Hoolahan was the first to notice that, at the advanced age of 10, I could not read or write a single solitary word. I was entirely illiterate. The 'softly softly' approach to my education in England had somehow contrived to overlook my education. I distinctly remember sitting in the English classroom when reading lessons came around. Everyone, including myself, would take out their books. I would watch my classmates read, and turn the pages at the same time as they did. Sitting beside my pal, Keith Walker, I would laugh at funny passages at the same time he did. I think Keith had me sussed out, as he gave me curious looks on many an occasion, and no doubt began to laugh at nothing to confirm his own suspicions, but the teachers were far easier to fool. As far as they were concerned, I could read. But I could not.

I was a proper little conman, never realising that I was conning myself. Dear Miss Hoolahan, however, took the situation in hand, and with the help of Sesame Street, taught me to read and write faster than you can say 'Jack Robinson'.

It was a liberating experience like no other, and I began to feel on a par with my peers for the first time. It was of course, too late to save me from the agonies I would endure up until then, when, on my birthdays, my friends would show up with nothing but books to bestow upon my clueless young self. I would have to keep up the pretence that I could in fact read, and act all delighted when presented with gems like Sir Walter Scott's 'Ivanhoe!'.

I had a fine teacher in fifth class called Mr Brennan. He was an ornithologist par excellence, and passed on his love of birds to his little charges. He also gave me great encouragement in the art department. I produced many a mini masterpiece, depicting blue tits on bottle tops, and under his guidance I created my finest piece of work up to that point. A scene from 'Jaws' fashioned from plasticine and crepe paper.

It was a fairly graphic representation of the moment when Robert Shaw's character slides slowly down the deck in the waiting jaws of our eponymous hero, and it caused quite a sensation in that terrific little school. It was put on display for all to see, and all of a sudden, I was an artist of great renown.

Yes indeed, St Connaire's was good to me, but my homesick mum was soon to get her way, and my perfect little existence came to a shuddering halt. After experiencing such educational delights, I'm sure you can imagine what it was like to be suddenly thrust into the grasping hands of a demonic shower of cloak clad sadists.

Most troubling of all is the fact that there are huge gaps in my memory from that time. I firmly believe that I deliberately brought this about, or that the trauma caused me to employ some form of natural sanity saving device. But the brothers did not defeat me, and the fact that I still have a very strong English accent is testament to that. I remain an Irishman with an English accent just to spite them. The brothers came and went, to Hell, with any luck, and our family was about to experience its worst trauma up til then, my dear dad's first heart attack. He would normally commute alone, from Shannon to Dublin and back in time for work on Monday. But as luck would have it, my big sister was with him on this occasion, and she saved his life.

At thirteen, I was still too young to grasp the brevity of the situation, but I shall never forget that day. We nearly lost our dad. Had that happened, our family would have been destroyed forever, and the future would have been very different.

He was the rock that held everything together, and a shining beacon in all our lives. As Oscar Wilde might have said, to lose him would have been careless, but to us, it was unthinkable. Many people are given to waxing lyrical about their paters, but my dad fully deserved the plaudits.

There was never a more diplomatic man, for starters. How he dealt with the voracious volatility displayed by us, his offspring, on a daily basis was nothing short of miraculous, but it was his spiritual side, and his intellect, that had me in a permanent state of awe.

He was classically educated and bandied many's the Latin phrase about in the most amusing of fashions, particularly at the dinner table. He was learned and articulate and never once did he use foul language, which was miraculous when you consider the expletive driven nature of Irish society. He shared my appreciation of football, and shall we say, the finer aspects of the female form.

He rose to a high position in the world of business, and provided a comfortable life for us all, so thanks Big Sis, your quick thinking actions on that cold winter's night in 1977 enabled us to enjoy the company of this remarkable man for many more years to come.

It was a massive attack, that first one, and his recuperation was slow and painstaking. I remember many hospital visits, and my dad weakly saying "Good man" to me as I stood by his bed. He got stronger, with the help of some marvellous medical people, and before we knew it, we were waving goodbye to Ray and Sandra, to Geraldine from next door, and pulling off in the car again. That happened a lot in my childhood, but I have no complaints. We were heading back to Shannon again and Julie Covington's mournful lament would soon be a distant memory.

Upon our return, we became domiciled in a part of Shannon called Tola Park. I quickly got settled in, and decided to explore my new neighbourhood. As I moseyed on down the road, at the far end of the park, I was two kids kicking a ball about.

Ah! Football! The great unifier! I approached the lads, and they graciously permitted my participation. After the kickabout, as is traditional, we sat on the kerb to swap witticisms. One of the kids told jokes straight out of The Beano, but myself and the other chap improvised, and made up some surreal, daft and meaningless stories.

"There was a bloke, you see, and he was walking own he road, and the moon fell on his head, which caused a giraffe in Mongolia to lose its spots" and so forth.

His name was Pascal, and we immediately discovered common ground. We fell about the place in great amusement. We sat and chatted til the sun went down, and little did we know, but the strongest bond of friendship ever enjoyed by man had just been formed by two young boys.

Pasc was 12, I was 13, and we were on the cusp of something truly enormous. We were to share all the ups, and all the downs of post adolescence together. Pascal was chiselled out of pure granite, stronger than twenty fully grown men and to top it all, he was a sensational footballer. He was grimly determined to do everything to the highest standard, and he succeeded. He never did anything by halves and had more mental energy than he could use, the surplus of which went in every direction imaginable. We owned the world for a couple of blissful years. It was all ours.

Nothing intruded on our friendship, and our bond was rock solid and we indulged ourselves in the holy trinity, the three things that truly mattered. Football, girls, and music.

So dear readers, we have come full circle again, let us put the age of innocence behind us, let us take that walk to school, and let us discover that dreaded ten pound note.

I should have returned that book money!

She was one of the loveliest girls I ever knew. She was an extraordinarily talented visual artist, but immensely modest too. Her eyes would bewitch any man. They were brown, but if you looked closely, you could see that they were made up of a composite of different colours that twinkled and changed all the time. Although we did become friends in later life, she would always remain romantically elusive, along with a vast proportion of her brethren.

Despite my love life grinding to a sudden halt when I got married in 1989, previous to that, I had never been short of girlfriends. Heady days indeed, but although I had enjoyed many the affiliation, I never felt secure about it. In those days, it was like asking a girl out, hearing her say "yes" and clinging on for dear life.

It was the age old story too, if I found a nice girl, it would never last as my mind was always on the unobtainable. I messed up so many times, it doesn't bear thinking about, much less writing about, and although I shall probably have to allude to my ill-fated marriage again, we will leave the subject of women behind for now, and move on to creatures of greater importance.

Basil the Wonderdog

Dogs, canines, pooches, or in the gaelic – an madraí, have always played a significant role in my life. In recent years, due to circumstances, other people's dogs have played a significant role in my life, but once upon a time, I was lucky enough to enjoy the company of man's best friend, exclusively, and all to myself. Out first family dog was a black lab called Cindy, who I believe, we inherited off our dear Aunt Diana, who is happily still with us, I hasten to add. Cindy, or was it Sindy?, went to live on a farm at a time when we were all still young enough to believe such nonsense. I do, however, clearly remember seeing her run up the stairs long after her supposed departure for pastures new. I kicked up a fuss about this apparition, which my astonished folks must have found quite unnerving.

In England we had many pets, gerbils, hamsters, guinea pigs, terrapins, cats, hedgehogs and the like, but our second ever dog was Tarzan. He was a big, batty, daft hound who was scared of cats and ate giant rocks. He was a great character, who I believe, eventually fell victim to poison deposited in a nearby field by irate farmers. It was either that, or his almost exclusive diet of rocks, which put paid to dear old Tarzan.

It wasn't until 1981 that my folks finally succumbed to my relentless pleading, and constant protestations that I was a man without a dog. I had the job in the printers, and I was in a position to pay for his upkeep, so why shouldn't I have one?

A man can achieve anything though persistent nagging, and I was soon to enjoy one of a multitude of treasured memories that involved my dad, as we went in search of something to shut me up. Word had it that a hound had become available in Hurlers Cross, a townland adjacent to Shannon, and we wasted no more time.

We went to meet a lad named James Morrisey, who led us to a shed with a worried look on his face. "He's in here" he said, and opened the door. "Wasn't the best of the litter" he explained, as we gazed down at what amounted to a big dollop of black hair. There was no mistaking it, it was an indistinguishable lump of immobility with a tail, and it didn't seem to be breathing.

"Not quite what we had in mind" said Pops, in his own understated and inimitable fashion, as he slipped James Morissey a fiver for his trouble. I scooped up the apparently coma stricken animal, laced him gingerly in the car, and accompanied my dad back to the ranch.

Over a period of a few weeks, with gentle encouragement, this peculiar little addition to our family came to life. First he wagged his tail, then he opened his eyes, then he started to eat like a horse! He had a lot of catching up to do, and right before my very eyes, Basil the Wonderdog was born!

In no time at all, he had metamorphosised into the most magnificent of beasts, with a handsome, noble countenance, set off by an immensely athletic build. His ears gave the impression that he had long silky black hair flowing around his irresistible face and his coat consisted of the shiniest, most healthy, substance, creating an overall impression of outstanding natural beauty. He was a knockout of the canine variety, and within a month, his journey from somewhat underwhelming puppyhood to unparalleled superiority was complete.

My dad had invested a fiver in what was obviously the world's most perfect dog. From 1981 til 1989, practically an entire decade, Basil was my most significant other, and mutual admiration abounded as we enjoyed the perfect relationship.

My constant companion at the best of times, Basil shone his light on me throughout a decade of decadence, unemployment, emigration and rampant insecurity.

I could holler "BASOOOO!" from any location in Shannon, no matter how far from our house, and within minutes, my best friend would be galloping towards me in a state of unbridled excitement. I swear he knew what day of the week it was, he understood every word I said and in his own way, could hold his own conversationally.

The state of this feckin' country during that dreadfully depressed decade forced me, periodically, to hightail it as far as England in search of work, and Basil stayed at home. Those were heart wrenching times, I can tell you. Eventually, after years of coming back and forth like a yoyo, I put forced emigration behind me, once and for all, and returned to Ireland for the final time, grimly determined to find work and settle down with Basil.

With a massive helping hand from my folks, I acquired my first property, enrolled in a government training scheme, and I was all set. Basil was nine, I guess, and approaching the prime of his life. I was looking forward to sharing his dotage with him, and we couldn't have been happier as we strolled around our favourite haunts, including the points, scenic areas at the mouth of the Shannon Estuary, just minutes from our new house. I was so relieved! I was home, reunited with the wonderdog, and the future was brimming with fresh possibilities.

Then one morning in March, 1989, I bid Basil farewell as it was time to go to the training course. "See you at lunch time" I said, and Basil walked off in the other direction, toward the point. This routine had been established quite quickly, Baz would take his morning constitutional, I would go to work, and we would meet for grub at lunch time back at the house. But on this occasion, upon my return, there was no sign of himself.

"Ah, he's probably found himself a lady friend" I said to myself, and carried on with the day. He would do that, you know, disappear for long periods, and come back half starved, but satisfied. He was free to do as he pleased, without restriction.

After a few days, however, I got a bad feeling, and began to worry. I searched fruitlessly, high and low, and employed search parties of local kids to help. Still no sign.

But on Paddy's Day, as I was at home, decorating with the help of my folks, as it happened, there was a knock on the door. I answered and one of the search parties stood on my step. By the looks on their faces, I could tell they had found Basil, and the news was not good. A young spokesman stepped forward, and the next words I heard were his.

"We found your dog, mister."

As it turned out, another local kid had witnessed what had happened, and he led the party to the spot Basil had been discovered partly submerged in the mud of the riverbank. He had obviously run into the river in an attempt to escape from his assailants, but it was too late, as he was already mortally wounded. The young witness said he saw a pack of dogs attacking our defenceless friend, egged on by a bunch of fellas with shotguns. These lowlife examples of what passes for humanity were known for such things, Basil being just the latest in a long line of victims. They call themselves hunters, and employ hunting dogs, which they keep locked in sheds for weeks on end, before unleashing them on anything unfortunate enough to move.

Basil had been murdered in cold blood, and my whole world had come tumbling down. The short life of a dog, perhaps, would not shake the world to its foundations, and it certainly didn't make the news when he passed away, but a dog offers unique friendship, ceaseless loyalty and indispensable comfort to their human compatriots. Only fellow dog lovers could have understood my response to the wonderdog's demise, as I shed rivers of tears for two solid weeks.

Strangely, the grief experienced at the loss of an animal is so utterly profound that it far exceeds grief felt at the loss of a member of our own species. Thankfully, I was not going to endure anything comparable to it for many years to come.

I still see Basil regularly. He is a frequent guest star in my dreams. Always there, ever present, frolicking in the summer meadows of a world conjured up in my subconscious. He has not died yet, for he is a part of me. When I die, he is coming with me, or I'll kick up a fuss! We shall always be together. We were once a single entity, and shall remain so forever.

Like every member of his species, Basil possessed an intelligence, an intuition, and an enormous capacity to love that is generally underestimated by mere humans. If we, as a race, displayed even a fraction of the qualities, then the 'dog eat dog' tendencies intrinsic in our psyche would be merely, and unfairly, applicable only to dogs themselves.

Marriage

During the search for Basil, I had occasion to bump into a girl from my youth.

Being a girl from my youth, she was, inevitably, someone who I had a major crush on, as there were very few lucky enough to escape my attentions. Upon this occasion, she kindly enquired as to whether Basil had been found, and when I replied in the negative she graciously sympathised, and I walked her home.

She was always, in my own estimation, way out of my league, and I didn't labour under any romantic illusions at the time, for she was a creature of unsurpassed physical beauty, and I was, in my own estimation, quite the opposite. But circumstances contrived to have us meet again, and I thought I sensed a spark, so after a period of agonised deliberation, I finally found the courage to ask her out. Moments later, we were married, we had a beautiful son, and we were headed for a quickfire divorce!

In reality, these events took two and a half years to unfold, but looking back now, they went by in the blink of an eye. To put it simply - I adored the ground she walked on, but the feeling was far from mutual. Breaking up was hard to do, but all things happen for a reason, and some for the greatest reason of all. Procreation.

I still have treasured memories of the marriage, despite everything. The day itself was absolutely brilliant. I had the time of my life, and I would recommend it to anyone. I was a proud man that day, and I am grateful for it, however short-lived out union ultimately proved to be.

I was also lucky enough to witness my baby son's overwhelming delight on two Christmas mornings, and every day in between, for he was an unbelievably happy little fella.

Strange though it may seem, the wee lad never cried. Even when he was teething, he just grunted a little. Clandestine feeding sessions where he would literally engulf bottle after bottle stick in my memory, and the natural creation of an unbreakable father-son bond makes that time very precious to me. We were not destined to live together in a family unit, but that bond remained just as strong throughout the years and I have been blessed with a wonderful son. I scarcely deserve such a thing, but I am not giving him back.

Yes, Shane, it's time to squirm with embarrassment, as you have reached the page where I get terribly sentimental and begin to sing your praises from the rooftops. I didn't think it was possible, but you have replaced Basil as my significant other, and my only complaint is that you don't seem to be like the other kids. You have never given me a hard time!

He's all grown up now, is our kid. He's a physics graduate and he lives in Cork with his lovely girlfriend. He gave me great encouragement when I told him I was embarking upon this book's creation, and he offered to type the whole thing out into manuscript form!

How about that? They don't come any better!

Is this quite what you were expecting, Shaybo? No? Well, that makes two of us, old buddy.

So far, it has been a succession of bewildering concentric circles, as an editor, there isn't much you can do about that, but I appreciate your efforts so far.

To prove my point, I am back in the doctor's waiting room, coming full circle again. It is like the black hole of Calcutta in here today, or the return of the bubonic plague. It seems someone has stolen our air supply. We are just a wheezing, gasping, breathless heap of pathetic humanity and forgive me my son and editor if what you are reading reflects this.

A large Russian bloke has just started gibbering, in an alarming, delirious fashion, into his mobile phone. Which just about sums up the mood, herein! If that makes any sense, and if it does not, edit at will, my boy, edit at will!

(*Editors note: I have kept the author's writing largely intact, just fixing some spelling and separating the babble into paragraphs. Beyond that, if I have to suffer, everyone has to suffer, so read on and enjoy.*)

The 1980s?

I do apologise, and I shall do my darndest to restore
equilibrium as I continue with the memoirs of a
chronic amnesiac! Armed with an updated doctor's
certificate, I am back at the coffee shop, a venue
most conducive to writing, so I have no excuses.
Copious quantities of the bean may counteract the
effects of yet another sleepless night.
This vicious, virulent, unrelentingly ghastly cold is
proving harder to shift than previously anticipated
and on various occasions last night I beseeched the
almighty powers that be to come and release me from
my agonising earthly coil. They ignored me, once
again, I dare say because I am yet to finish my
memoirs, and there is much work to be done.
Night time terrors, such as last nights, do however,
cause me to ponder upon the nature of flu viruses
and how implicitly nasty they actually are. Why do
they attack you when you are lying down? Removing
every breath from your body and replacing it with
unutterable ticklish irritation of the throat? Is it
because you are more vulnerable when you are
prostrate within your scratcher?
You have beaten me, thy foul and merciless
bacterium. I am defeated, I have no fight left. You

win. Any chance you could move onto the next poor bastard?

I think perhaps I am prevaricating on this occasion for a reason. We have, after all, reached that dreaded decade, the 1980s, and the prospect of attempting to write anything remotely chronological is a little daunting, to say the least. They were very eventful years, even if they were blighted by maudlin melancholia. The never ending search for security through work was the overriding theme, and I found myself employed in many ventures.

The short lived dream job in the printers, ANCO (a government body) training schemes of various description in which I read a lot of classic literature deep within the bowels of the gentleman's conveniences, working for a fella called Mick Ring in his engineering shop, driving trains for London Transport, enduring hellish conditions in assorted English sweat shops, and even working for a while as a stable lad in the picturesque county of Worcestershire. Just a few of the things I did in a jam-packed decade when all I really wanted was to wander about in forests with Basil.

I cannot remember dates and times with any sort of accuracy, and when I try to do so, events appear to overlap each other, giving an overall impression of retrospective time travel.

My dad was managing a company in Shannon called Befab throughout the 80s, and without his intervention, I would not have found work here at all. He subcontracted some work out to a fella called Mick Ring, who in return, took a giant leap, and employed me. I remember showing up in a suit for the interview, and Mick giving out because to work in his shop, a chap needed to be attired in a set of overalls!

He was only a few years older than me, but way ahead of me in every other respect. He was an extraordinarily driven man, always flying about at break-neck speed in pursuit of his business activities. I worked a couple of years in his company L&B Engineering, before emigrating, or something such as that. But for years after that, if you were stuck, Mick would always give you a start, whether he had the work or not. He was that kind of bloke. Having succumbed to an illness some years ago, Mick is no longer with us, but he will always be a hero to me. He took the whole company out nearly every Friday for a pint, and was the personification of generosity. When Ireland reached the quarter finals of the World Cup in 1990, myself and my beloved ex-boss did a jig of delight, hand in hand, on a table in the Shannon Knights, a local watering hole in which I spent many a lost weekend. That was Mick Ring, a true local legend.

My dad's company, somewhat controversially at the time, manufactured aircraft arresting systems for the military wings of various governments. It was a thriving operation in its day, and my dad often had me accompany him to his office, where he would show me around, demonstrating the company's procedures.

The company closed some years ago, but the building is still there, right across the road from my house. There are many other old, out of use factory buildings around there too. It is an eerie experience, taking a walk down there. It was once humming with human activity, but now it is a derelict ghost estate. If you look in the window of Befab, you can see my dad's old office, and the canteen, which still has cups and old milk bottles scattered about on the tables, as if the staff just suddenly vanished in an instant. All that industry, all the sweat and tears, suddenly grinding to a halt. I am overwhelmed with nostalgia upon those walks.

The building still exists as a monument to my dad's enterprise, but to gaze upon it in its present state of neglect is a very painful thing.

There was no room for hangers on in our house back then, and if you found yourself unemployed and unable to contribute, you were invariably awoken with a thud by the early morning jabberwocks and kicked out with an unceremonious boot up yer arse, to pound the cold and lonely pathways of the local industrial estates until you managed to at least nag your way into the office of one of the many personnel officers, who would stare at you blankly, furnish you with a form, and bid you a cursory farewell.

Long periods of unemployment, however, were not tolerated, and if you couldn't find a job it was off to England with you, my son! It was a case of out sight, out of mind, as my unwanted self joined the hordes of other unfortunates who had lingered under the feet of their folks for long enough, masses of Ireland's great unwashed bid farewell to the old sod and headed for an uncertain future in dear old Blighty. When I first arrived in London, I went straight to an Irish centre in search of accommodation. A very helpful geezer gave me an address in Kilburn and said "Go find this house, and ask for Kathleen". I eventually found it, and sure enough, an archetypal, if aging, Irish cailín called Kathleen Moriarty, from the hills of Kerry, no less, answered the door. She made a terrible fuss of me on the doorstep before letting me in.

Kathleen was a great woman, and just the tonic for a lost lamb like myself, freshly off the boat. It turned out she was the landlady of a large hostel, called St Brendan's, and this was it, my first address away from home. It was a decrepit old construction, rather like Kathleen herself, populated with a motley collection of Irish men, some who had lived there for decades, and some had, like myself, just landed. There were communal dormitories, in which crowds of us slept, a TV room in which we sat of an evening, and a kitchen in which Kathleen was known for getting randy over the morning cornflakes. (It was very educational.)

I went to Baker Street, just sightseeing, about 3 days after settling in to St. Brendan's and noticed that London Underground were having a recruitment drive at the station. I went to investigate, and within minutes, I was their latest recruit. I signed my name and hey presto! I was a bona fide member of a highly respected institution.

I was given a cap and uniform, in which I looked most dapper, it has to be said, and sent off to training college in White City, near Shepherd's Bush. Training took nine weeks. It was very intensive, and thorough, and I loved every minute of it. I was in college at last! I had made it!

I graduated, and set to work on my first train, as a guard. A love-hate thing soon developed, and pretty soon I wasn't sure what aspects of the job I loved, and which I hated. I stuck it out, and I was training as a driver when outside influences got the better of me, and I packed it all in.

I left St Brendan's when a few of the ignorant bogtrotters there resident became too much to deal with, a situation which culminated in a drunk old git mistaking my bed for a toilet during the night, and I moved into a squat with some of my pals from Ireland. We were an unruly bunch, given to drinking a lot. My discipline deserted me, and I let the underground job slip out of my hands. Things became fractured, there was a lot of messing, and misplaced loyalty. Looking back, I should have kept it together. That was a damn good job, but destiny had other ideas.

We were young, and we had wild oats to sow. I figure we squatted in an assortment of establishments for a couple of years, and went our separate ways after that, but it is a blurry period in my memory. I remember a feeling of unsettle insecurity over taking me, and that was to prove fairly unshakable over the coming years. I could not get a foothold, and moved all over England, and back to Ireland, numerous times, all the time listening to my predominant musical obsession, The Smiths, on my Walkman. Man! Who can get a handle on the eighties!?

I do remember getting my fill of London. It seemed a most inhospitable place to me. Gazillions of folk milling about and not one would stop for a chat. If anonymity is what you seek, it is the perfect spot for you, but in those days I was still a sociable creature, and I found the big city to be something of an isolating place.

I worked as a postman near Camberwell at one stage and enjoyed that job immensely. It kept me very fit, as there appeared to be a terrific amount of letters to deliver on a daily basis! I got a tip off from another postie at the end of one particularly long day as I sat, knackered, back in the sorting office. "Paddy" he said "they're taking the piss out of you, mate." It seemed I had been delivering the loads of another postman, a cheeky little English chappy, all along. He sat drinking tea in the depot as I toiled with his enormous bag of crap.

I had been doing the work of two postmen, and they had all been having a good old laugh at the dumb Irishman's expense. Cheeky Charlie wasn't laughing after I got wind of it, mind you. He himself became a laughing stock after he found himself inside a large delivery bag, in the back of a van bound for Scotland. I always found myself in a unique position, being an Irishman with an English accent. I am discriminated against in equal measure in both countries, but it must be said, I have had a far worse time in England. I once worked for a fanatical nationalist in Limerick, who once had a hissy fit when he found me reading an English paper in the canteen, but on the whole working in England left me more consistently marginalised.

The worst job I ever had was in an industrial printer's in Sussex, where I was treated despicably by a brigade of anti-Irish gobshites. I remember being at the company 'Do' one Christmas, and after about three hours of trying to communicate with my 'colleagues' it slowly dawned on me that I was being deliberately ignored.

There was a block there who I thought I could relate to, as he was friendly enough at work, so I approached him and said "no-one's talking to me here, man." He proceeded to ignore me too, obviously

afraid to be seen communicating with the Paddy.
What these people didn't realise of course, was that I
was born about three miles down the road from the
Christmas 'Do' venue!

Ironic, innit? Har har! Sidney has the last laugh!
That was a terrible job, though, and I have used it as
a yardstick ever since. Nothing could possibly get
that bad again. It was physically exhausting
relentless toil, pure slavery, in fact. You were barely
allowed a toiled break and my supervisor was a sub-
human monster who kept telling me how he would
one day be a millionaire and – "You will always be a
navvy, Paddy" to paraphrase the little prick!

Yes indeed, there is a peculiar breed of bigot at large
in England and although everyone is wonderful, as
we established earlier in this book, some of my
English co-workers were not!

Being Anglo-Irish has not affected my sense of
identity as my life experience has been
predominantly Irish, and I have to admit, the
English, and the society they inhabit, are a mystery
to me. It is probably down to me, and how I perceive
things, but they seem to be a sadly insular race,
reluctant even to mix with themselves, never mind
anyone else. They appear to be a massive collection

of individuals, perfectly lovely individuals, I am sure, but they lack unity, from where I'm sitting.

Had we not boarded The Munster car ferry all those years ago, I might well have ended up sitting here saying the same thing about the Irish. The colour of our blood does indeed define us, but at the end of the day, the fundamental differences between our two nations are hard to define, and we share large parts of our culture. Our music, our television, our films and our art. And so ends this tedious trawl through Anglo-Irish relations as the end of this page has mercifully just arrived.

Mississippi

It has just dawned on me! The reason I left the job
with L&B engineering was indeed Emigration. I went
to America, to seek my fortune!
When we were kids, our Uncle Bob would
occasionally pay us a visit. He was a larger than life
American and we all adored him. His generosity was
legendary. He would hand us ten pound notes and
boom in his uniquely jolly way – "Go get some candy,
kids!" and there was always great excitement when
he was around. He was your proverbial favourite
uncle, and my dad's older brother, which gave him
an exalted position in the grand scheme of things.
He would often say "You kids come see yer Uncle Bob
anytime now, y'hear? Always plenty of room at our
house." And the atmosphere he created was always
lighthearted, sincere, and Uncle Bobbly benevolent.
My own brother had already headed to Bob's
homestead, in Pascagoula, Mississippi come 1985,
and I decided that I wanted my own shot at the
American dream. So I announced to all and sundry
that I was leaving Eireann's golden shores to seek
pastures new, that I would probably never be back,
and you had better take care of Basil, or there will be
trouble. I gave in my notice at work, attended a

farewell bash, and set out, with some trepidation, for a new life.

I duly arrived in New York, planning to spend some time there with my kid sister and some pals before heading south. I had saved five hundred books prior to leaving and promptly had the whole lot lifted from my back pocket while engaged in the act of playing pool. Not clever! Quite dumb, in fact, and not the most auspicious start to my American adventure.

It wasn't the best two weeks, but it was never dull. On one occasion I found myself sleeping in Central Park, being harassed by uncompromising cops, and imploring passers-by to lend me fifty cents to get on the subway. I could easily have ended up among the huge New York bum population. But I somehow managed to get to New Orleans, I think I got the bus, but don't ask me how, and I called my dear old Uncle Bob, ready to move in, to start working in his legendary shrimp business, and t start my journey to millionairiness.

But that's not quite how it worked out.

My job entailed beating catfish to death with a club before feeding them to crabs, which were duly fattened up and sold in Bob's shop. Pascagoula was the biggest shock of all. Stifling heat, humidity, and a cold, barren, unforgiving landscape. Mosquitoes, bull frogs, crickets, and ants abounded, and culturally, it was living within a farfetched Arthur Haley novel. Inhospitable does not begin to describe it. I hoped to see my cousin Trish, as I was staying with her mom and dad quite near Bob's homestead (Uncle Brian and Aunt Phyllis, wonderful folk who had just moved there themselves), but I never did see Trish, as she was in Kentucky, having signed up with the Marines!

My American dream was turning into a nightmare, and it began to dawn on me that Uncle Bob's invitations to come visit were meant to be taken with a pinch of salt. Dreams and reality were suddenly, and sadly, easily distinguishable. I was given to writing letters and such in those days, and one day, sing lashings of poetic license, it has to be said, I wrote one such letter home, to my pal Murph, to be precise.

I described my circumstances, and didn't hold back. The letter was not a flattering evaluation of my dear relatives, and needless to say, it never made it as far as Murph. It fell into the wrong hands, and before I knew it, I was back on the old sod, tail between the legs, begging good old Mick Ring to give me my job back.

Getting home wasn't easy, but I was never so glad to see Basil! I was just a dumb greenhorn kid who hadn't got a bull's notion, entrusting my fate to something I was never sure of, and living life on a wing and a prayer. Uncle Bob sadly passed away many years ago, and I never had a chance to make it up to him. He was just being himself, and he was entitled to do that, he didn't deserve the disparaging things I said about him.

I got carried away with the creative prose while composing that infamous letter, and I was never able to explain that to him. I loved my Uncle Bob, as did my dad, and dad was always a good judge of character. My American cousins recently informed me that that letter still exists and on occasions it is brought out to be read aloud to invited company. My reputation on those shores is assured for life, and I shall never live it down.

Mississippi still exists in time warp, with segregation in all but law, and ignorant rednecks flying about in pickup trucks spouting obscenities. The only thing on the telly is the Brady Bunch, repeated on an endless loop, and my cousins may well be still sitting there under the air conditioner, staring blankly at something known only to themselves.

The most bizarre thing of all was an experience I upon my return. I had spent a frenetic, deranged and alcohol soaked month in America, and what with the heat and the incredible racked created by various creatures of the night, I don't think I slept a solitary wink. When I got home, I must have headed straight for bed. Heaven knows how long I must have slept, but when I awoke, I had absolutely no idea where I was, or where I had been. I awoke in a dark room, completely at a loss to account for my situation.

I might have had a combination of jetlag and the DTs, because I just lay there in stupefied shock, completely oblivious to my surroundings, listening to a shrill whirring sound that seemed to emanate from outside. Tripping and hallucinating, I got up to investigate. I pulled the curtain. There was my dad, mowing the lawn! I started banging on the window, intensely freaked, and calling out – "Oy! You! Who are you! What's that noise! Stop it! Go away!"

It was the strangest moment of my young life. I did not know where I was. I did not know who I was. I did not know who my dad was. I completely lost it and kept banging on the window until my dad came in and brought me back down to Earth. He just smiled and said "You've been dreaming Son. It's ok." But Lord only knows what he must have thought when he first saw his lunatic son upon his return from the 'Mericas.

The veritable Mick Ring gave me my job back, but things were not going well for his company, and it was soon to close. Mick set up a smaller operation, and like I said, he was always gracious enough to give me a start of it if I was stuck, but I figured it was time to move on, being once again afflicted with the itchy feet.

Sometime later, I found myself in the most agreeable of places, a town beyond compare, the magnificent and ancient City of Tribes, that which is GALWAY, on the west coast. These days, with the advent of roads, and the introduction of public transport, it is an easily accessible place, and can be reached in no time at all, but back then, it still seemed like a remote and far off spot, shrouded in Gaelic mystery, and the only way to reach it was to hitch hike. Yes, I am talking about the 1980s here. We are discussing the West of Ireland, and back then, uncivilised though it may have been, it still had some rustic charm.

Galway was absolutely brilliant. Still, in my humble estimation, the greatest town on Earth, even if it is overpopulated these days. I brought Basil with me, he was a mean hitch hiker, in fact, and we quickly got settled in. I signed on the dole, for there was no work to be had, and we moved into rooms above a pub. Strictly speaking, there were no dogs allowed, but Basil the wonderdog was adept at canine subterfuge, and we managed to sneak upstairs through a crowded pub, undetected, on a daily basis, and join our little gang upstairs.

I loved that gang. We were tight, and we looked out for one and other. I got 40 punts a week on welfare, twenty of which went on rent, and ten of which covered Basil's pedigree chum, and ten of which had to stretch in many other directions. Money did not matter, however, it was not an issue, as fresh air was free, and fresh air existed in abundance above in the City of Tribes.

We spent our days on Salthill Beach, braced by the chill Atlantic breeze and many the evening wandering the streets of that wonderful town. I was just a blow-in, of course, but I felt a great affinity with that place, and a fierce sense of belonging. It was steeped in history, populated by the most excellent of people, and it was an entirely unpretentious location. It was real!

If only I could have found a job! If I had done so, life would have been complete, but this was still the 1980s, and there was nothing to be had. I eventually got on to another training scheme, where I became part of another tight little unit, befriending folk that I shall never forget. It was freezing in winter, and rained consistently all year round, but those couple of years were certainly worthwhile. Sadly however, Basil Bond's cover was eventually blown, and we had to move out.

We visited the folks back in Shannon, who convinced me that I couldn't fart around in Galway with Basil forever, and it was time to clamber upon that banana boat again, and head for Blighty.

A terrible event took place while I was on that training course, and we lost our cousin Trish. We had grown up together, first in England, and then in Shannon. She was an unforgettable girl, with charisma to burn, and we had been in all sorts of scrapes together. Her passing cast a pall over me, and intruded forever into the perfection of life in Galway. I was resigned once again to emigrate.

Sussex

My parents valiantly attempted to resolve the
question of 'What to do About Kevin?' by arranging
for me to go and stay with my Uncle Pat and Aunt
Pauline in Sussex. Despite being warned that Kevin
was a "Dope-head who never did an honest day's
work in his life" by other well-meaning relatives, Pat
and Pauline, out of the goodness of their hearts,
agreed to take me on.

I was to meet my brother, and we were to go directly
to Sussex from the airport. This seemed like a good
plan, until I was asked to fill out an address form on
the plane. It was part of strict anti-terrorism
procedures in place at the time, and I figured I had
better not make up some fictitious address, and as I
didn't know my exact destination, I was forced to
leave that part of the form blank.

This came to the notice of the authorities upon my
arrival, and I was asked to join them in a rather
intimidating little interrogation room which was
comprised of a table, and three chairs. I occupied
one of the chairs, and two chaps occupied the other
two. They were not overly friendly, which was
unfortunate, as I was to share that room with them
for the next twelve hours while my brother sat

wondering where I was, and my Uncle Pat and his good wife became more than a little concerned.

I was grilled like a bewildered sardine while the anti-terrorism squad examined every item I had in my possession, most crucially of which was my diary at the time. A huge compendium which detailed all sorts of unsavoury activities carried out by yours truly.

"I wasn't sure of my destination. I left the form blank coz I was meeting my brother at the airport, and we were going to my Uncle's together" I said. "It's the truth. Why don't you page my brother? He's out there waiting for me" and they repeatedly ignored me, the plonkers. I think they must have really enjoyed reading my diary, as they appeared to be well engrossed in it. Perhaps it provided a diversion from the tedium of their everyday lives.

Finally, they paged Maurice, and I went to meet his somewhat emotionally exhausted self. I wouldn't have blamed my brother had he formed a negative opinion of me over the years, as I have certainly given him plenty of reason, but thankfully, as far as I know, he hasn't.

I hadn't even arrived at my uncle's yet, and already I had put him and his lovely wife through the proverbial mill. It wasn't the last I'd hear from the

British special branch either, as they called to the house some six months later, just to check up on me, and gave my poor aunt the shock of her life in the process, the plonkers.

I think I lasted around 18 months in Sussex, it was the best of times, and the worst of times, for a myriad of unforgettable reasons. I never quite got over the unease created by the arrival debacle, but my uncle and aunt could not have been more accommodating when I finally arrived. The welcome I received still brings a tear to my eye as I ponder it over a cup of tea here in Skycourt, in the Shannon Town Centre.

I have been coming here every day for almost a fortnight, and it has brought home to me in great clarity the absolute folly of my recent self-imposed solitary confinement. It has made me realise that I still have a lot of dear friends hovering about, and it is most life affirming to discuss the ups and downs of this life them over tea.

My doctor tells me I have the flu. It is the real McCoy, and has left me quite in tatters, but my inability to work has thrust me once again out into the world. I realise that it is a friendly place, populated by folk just like myself, and I would like to think that my exile is over. I shall embrace society,

111

and the good people within it, from this moment on, for I am blessed to live in a country such as this, with the inbuilt amenable nature of its populace.

It was in 1988 that I was resident in Burgess Hill, Sussex, with my fantastic relatives, Pat, Pauline and their three little boys. I can recall the year as it contained a famous date in Irish folklore. A crowd had assembled in the front room to watch Ireland play England in a footy match. It was during the European Championship finals in Stuttgart, Germany and there was great excitement and anticipation throughout both our lands as the group gathered in Pat's house snuggled in to watch it. There were quite a few of us, and seats were of a premium, so I plonked my enormous frame on the arm rest at one end of the couch. There was a girl called Claire, if memory serves me right, sitting on the armrest at the other end, and a number of other folk comfortably planted between us. Claire had her leg in plaster, was using a crutch, and was perched quite precariously, but she seemed to be managing. That is until Ray Houghton famously stuck the ball in the English net! Because when this miracle occurred I jumped off my end of the couch and deprived it of the balance on which it depended. Its equilibrium was entirely upset, it rose up on one side, and poor Claire went tumbling off the other end. The poor thing lay there, replete with broken leg, as I ran about the house screaming hysterically. Of course, the English folk present among us did not find that one bit amusing.

I was a terribly insecure article in those days, and I could never quite shake off the idea that I was just an overgrown Irish imposition, even in the face of the never ending hospitality to which I was treated. Pauline always treated me to my favourite foods, nut roast, mushroom vol-au-vents and crispy salad It was heaven for a vegetarian, as up until then I had always felt like an awkward gastronomic minority. She also indulged me in my greatest passion, Scrabble, much to Pat's distaste, as he was something of an expert in Trivial Pursuit!

It was a wonderful interlude in my life, but being a lodger, I never felt comfortable in my own skin and could never really be myself. If I had it all to do again, I would surely fully embrace the love shown to me in that house. The three boys became like little brothers to me and those memories are very precious. There was quite an amount of drinking to be done, myself and Pat being O'Sullivans and all, and we fulfilled that obligation down in his local hostelry – Georgie's Disco Bar. A typically English joint during the 1980s, populated by vacant tarts and wannabe yuppies.

This is where I encountered the English at their vacuous worst, but also where I met my girlfriend at the time. Jenny was refreshingly liberal in her attitudes compared to the Catholic girls to which I had become accustomed, and being with her was always revelatory, to say the least. She was lovely, but as is always the case with me, her physical demands became a little tiresome. I liked to smoke a doobie, lay back, chill out and listen to The Smiths once in a while, and Jenny had some difficulty with that.

They were looking for a doorman down in our disco bar, and Pat kindly volunteered my services. It was a hell of a job, and I was way too soft, but I could hardly say no. Every Saturday night without fail, hordes of yobbos would descend on the place looking for a scrap with the big Irish bouncer. I got into some tight spots, but I lived to tell the tale.

Living there affirmed my Irishness, as English culture and I just did not mix, but looking back, it is a most precious period. Thank you Pat and Pauline. You and your terrific little lads will have a special place in my heart forever.

Work

It was in Sussex that I had the job from hell, and where I encountered rampant bigotry, and although it was a source of mild amusement to me most of the time, and I treated it with the indifference it deserved, I had my fill of it, and the job itself was murder.

Domestically, things were changing too, and I was desperate to attain some form of independence. I pissed off back to London, and squatted for a while. Christmas Day, 1988, was a low point. I was alone in a grotty squat, watching Eastenders on the box as misery unfolded all around me. I had a tin of Ambrosia creamed rice for dinner and a doobie for dessert. This is it, I thought, and resolved to return to Ireland, determined to exercise my right to be an Irish citizen at home.

Someone up there was, as ever, looking out for me, for when I returned, with the exception of Basil's horrendous departure, things began to fall into place. It was never easy, but I managed to find work in a number of places, before finding the occupation in which I am presently incumbent. It was 1991, and I was scouring local industries, as in days of yore, when I stumbled across a man who was to prove to be my saviour.

When I married in '89, I was fortunate enough to be employed in Westing House, Bay 7, a notable Shannon institution of the time. I loved that job, and I met some great people, but I hardly knew anyone as my wedding day approached. We got married, but we were skint, so a honeymoon was not an option. I went into work the Monday after the big day, and the guys in the canteen asked me "Well Kev. How was your weekend? Do anything exciting?" To which I answered, with great relish "Not really. I got married, if that counts?" Yes indeed. What a moment that was!

It was a temporary contract, and despite my pleading to be kept on, they let me go after six months, and I had to resume the old job hunting post-haste. I stumbled across a crowd called Expressair who overhauled aeroplanes in double quick time, and they gave me start. I was training with them, in fact, when I had the inestimable privilege of becoming a father bestowed upon me.

The training depot was right beside Befab, and my dad popped over one day with the news. He was his usual jovial self as he strolled in and imparted the important information. "She's gone into labour.

You're wanted in the hospital." "Oh. Alright Dad"
says I, and continued to rip covers off aircraft seats
as if nothing had happened. It really did not sink in,
until the trainer, a lad called Christy, came over to
me and said "You can stop doing that now, Kev. You
are going to be a daddy." I snapped out of it and
went outside. Sure enough, the Da was sitting in his
car, puffing his pipe, and laughing away at his shell
shocked son. We drove into town, Shaybo made his
entry into the world, and I was a made man!

That job soon took a turn for the incredible weird as I
was sent to a giant aircraft hangar in Holland to
begin work. They literally worked people to death
there. We worked from seven in the morning until
eleven at night, and then we would head to the bar
and drink til five! We were slaving our arses off,
sleeping for two hours, and starting all over again
without a break. Seven days a week!

I saw a bloke drop dead in front of me. He had
breathed in too much nitromorse, a paint-stripping
chemical, and copped it. I slept in a dorm with a
bunch of absolute nutters. Crazy alcoholics to a
man. They did this all the time, intensive work for a
few months, making big bucks, and then partying
like the clappers in Amsterdam for the rest of the
year.

After a few weeks of this, I looked like a cross between a werewolf and the abominable snowman. I never had a second to bite my nails, or to shave, and it's the one and only time I ever had a beard. The whole thing was bonkers, and it culminated one night when one of the leaders of the operation came into the dorm, pissed out of his skull, and started making passes at me as I lay in the bed.

I sat up, let him have it, (it wasn't what he wanted) and I was on a plane home the next day. They were shysters, and the whole thing stank of illegal practices.

I was greeted with total indifference when I got home, which didn't help. Where on Earth was I? How did I end up in such a place? Heaven knows, but I was there, and this was my lot. I at least had my baby boy, and I threw myself into daddyhood as another period of miserable unemployment began to take hold. I used to walk past this place in the industrial estate called 'Shannon Aircraft Motor Works' all the time. I looked in the window a couple of times, and thought to myself "That place looks very hi-tech. I'll never get a job in there." and I would go on my way, traipsing the darn streets in a never ending cycle of desperate futility.

Then one day, when I was up around that area again, I noticed a very distinguished looking Sikh gentleman getting out of his car. He approached the building, and I approached him. "I don't suppose there's any work going in there?" I asked. He nodded, benignly, and said "Come inside, we can discuss it." I relayed my situation to him. Recently married, just had a baby, things are looking a bit bleak. He said "Well. We can start you on Monday, if that is convenient." And little did I know, but that was the last time I was forced to walk the streets in search of work.

Paramjit Neote was a beautiful man to work for, as it turned out. An impeccably mannered gentleman who oozed spirituality from every pore in his skin. A wise man with a white beard and a turban who quickly joined Mick Ring on my list of heroic employers. He rescued me that day, and I am still employed in the company that he created, even if I have spent the past fortnight wandering the streets of Shannon like a plague stricken zombie with memoirs to write.

I can scarcely believe I have been employed by the same company for twenty-one years. I have seen a lot of ups and downs in that time, lean times, prosperous times, good times and bad. I have developed close friendships with so many people during that time, most notably a lady called Moira Kelly, who, as I have learned from previous experience, enjoys having her name mentioned in books!

So many people have come and gone in that time, it is nothing short of incredible. It is like home to me now, and the good people within it are my family. My beloved benefactors have demonstrated extraordinary patience, tolerance and understanding during my long tenure, and they have my eternal appreciation. Perhaps I should save the rest for my retirement speech, which is still a long way off, touch wood.

I have enjoyed this little break, for it has illustrated the fact that there is still life outside work, but I look forward to returning, for I am a part of something there, we have all been through hell and high water together, and I want to help man the pumps as we sail into what is always an uncertain future.

Flu

I enter another day as my influenza enters another stage. It is the 'cold sweat' phase, with some aching limbs thrown in for good measure. This must mean I am finally on the mend, and if I am not mistaken, I actually may have got some sleep last night, although it's hard to tell, as I might have been asleep at the time.

As it enters its final stages, I am already beginning to miss this flu. It has been with me for a long time, my constant companion through thick and thin, and it has opened up a whole new world to me. I often wondered what I would do if early retirement every reared its ugly head, now I know I could fit in with the other directionless souls who inhabit coffee shops during the day, and I could write silly books, such as this one.

I am grateful to the flu for bringing this truth home to me, thank you flu, for shedding a brighter light on what could possibly be my future. I forgive you for the sleepless nights and the indescribable agonies which accompanied them. The dry, retching cough, and the endless torment of the tickle in the throat! It seems that every cloud has a silver lining, as this book illustrates, and every supposed calamity does indeed lead to a bright new dawn.

I feel a guiding presence in my life. Today it is almost tactile. It may have arranged the flu for a reason, if so, I have to say, it was a bit extreme. But I understand the motive behind it, so, so be it, and thank you.

My Name

This might be a good time to clear up any confusion I may have created with regard to my moniker. I am aware that the reader may be aware of the fact that I have referred to myself by two different names during the composition of this rambling and apparently unidentifiable article. I dare say both 'Kevin' and 'Sidney' have appeared since its inception in Somerset. There are still small pockets within the confines of Shannon Town where I am referred to as 'Gordon' and quite a number of old school friends still call me 'Fonzy', but these are other stories, to which we may return.

I was christened Kevin O'Sullivan while Jagger gyrated inside the old telly, and that was my one and only name during my formative years. But my formative years were spent in England, and the English cannot pronounce the name Kevin without putting a terribly sharp emphasis on the letter I. Indeed, when a person of English extraction utters the name, to my ears, it is like someone running their nails across blackboards resident within my brain. My ears were constantly assaulted with this during childhood and I grew to despise the name Kevin as a result.

I have no memory of coming up with the name Sid, but my brother swears I got it from Sid James, the great old English actor, who a common sight on the telly in those days. I just stopped answering to Kevin and insisted that people call me Sid, much to the displeasure of my dear mother.

It stuck, and to this day I am referred to as Sid by the majority, although plenty, including most of my workmates, call me Kevin. I don't mind it so much when it is pronounced in a soft Irish lilt. It sounds like 'Keven' and is music to my ears.

I visited my folks in Wicklow one day, some years back, and we decided to go for a drive through the immense majesty of the mountains. "Let's go to Glendalough" says the Da, and it was agreed. I only had a vague idea of the significance of Glendalough at the time, and when we got there, I couldn't quite believe it. Breath-taking beauty abounded in every direction, it was paradise, and it left me totally stunned. The Ma, Da, and meself sat for a while to take it all in, and this is what my father told me – "Saint Kevin was a monk who wanted to build a monastery in the perfect place. He walked the length and breadth of Europe in search of the right spot. He was looking for something that resembled Heaven, and he found it here. He built his monastery and became a hero to the peasantry hereabouts. He taught them how to be self-sufficient, and single handedly erased poverty from their lives. This is Heaven, Kevin, and that is why I named you Kevin." In that instant, I longed to erase Sidney from history, but I was stuck with it. After sharing that amazing moment with my folks, I bear the name Kevin with pride.

If you haven't been to Glendalough, people, get thee hence! It is a humbling experience like no other and gives a person a sense of their place in the world. The achievements of this wandering monk from the Sixth Century will leave you awestruck, and his monastery, the round towers, and surrounding buildings will knock your socks off. It is exactly as he left it all those centuries ago. Man can return to the roots of his soul there, without any interruption from the modern world, with its infernal gizmos and pop culture crap.

Folk can feel a palpable affinity with their ancestry as the spirit of those bygone souls inhabits the very air you breathe, and a great peace descends upon you. I felt St. Kevin calling to me across the centuries, and I found my ultimate spiritual hero. Thank you St. Kevin, and once again, thank you, Dad!

Back in the 70s, before we went to Dublin, being domiciled in the Wesht of Ireland meant we only had one TV channel. It didn't come on until six in the evening and its itinerary consisted of farming programmes and current affairs on the whole, with occasional gem such as 'Hall's Pictorial Weekly' thrown in. But when we went to Dublin, we had a new-fangled gadget called the piping which meant we could get all the English channels! This was a marvellous thing, and we were all delighted.

My favourite show at the time was 'Happy Days' because I was fascinated by all that 50s rock n' roll, the quiffs, and the jukebox jiving, man! I thought Arthur Fonzerelli was the coolest thing since sliced bread and I wanted to be him. So, upon our return to Shannon, realising that nobody in one channel land had heard of him, I decided to steal his identity and I announced to all and sundry – "I am Arthur Fonzerelli. You can call me Fonz. I'm cool, man." And the naïve young one channel landers there assembled fell for it, hook line and sinker.

So for a very long time, I was known simply as Fonzy, (which was not all that uncommon a name down in the bog, as it happened, it being a variation of Alphonse) and quite a few around these here parts still refer to me as such.

Gordon came about quite by accident when I first moved to Lee Park, the house I let go in order to purchase the flat. I was kicking a ball about with some of the local kids just after I moved in. I did myself a terrible injury, spraining my ankle, and fell to the ground, exclaiming – "Oh. Gordon Bennett! Me leg" which is a throwback to the days of my childhood, for back then "Gordon Bennett" for reasons I have yet to fathom, was used as a kind of mild expletive.

The kids thereabouts started calling me Gordon after that, and now, if I stroll down to that neighbourhood, some of those kids, now grown up, still salute me with greetings such as "Well Gordon!", "Fancy a game of footy, Gordon?" and the like.

So, if I was to stroll around Shannon on any given day, I am likely to be hailed by passing folk who refer to me by four completely different appendages.

Sid, Kev, Fonz and Gordon.

This can be quite confusing, but I have yet to develop an identity crisis! If you think about it, it's kind of quaint, but my mum would never approve, bless her. So if you should ever bump into me, and I am in the company of my mum, be sure to call me Kevin.

The Diary

Many moons ago, in the early eighties, my dad had occasion to find himself in Heathrow Airport, during one of his frequent business trips, no doubt. There he stumbled upon one of my all-time heroes, a comedy genius without rival in my eyes, the incomparable Mr Spike Milligan. Now, anyone familiar with this untouchable behemoth of the entertainment world will know that he was a chronically shy, retiring sort of fella who shunned public scrutiny at all costs, but my dad must have worked his legendary charm on him, for they ended up having quite a cosy little chat.

During this chat, the following exchange took place.

Dad – "Ah, Spike. My son is a big fan of yours. Did you know he has read all your books?"

Spike – "Well, I never! Fame at last!"

My father went on to ask him for his autograph, and although by all accounts he rarely did so, he obliged. When he got home, my dad sought me out, relayed the story to me, and presented me with the autograph. By Jiminy, what a specimen it was! It looked as if the great man had spent hours creating it, with intricate lines and all sorts of fancy additions. It was the holy grail, and it belonged to me, little Sid Sullivan, of Shannon, Ireland.

It was the greatest treasure I could ever possess, and way beyond my wildest dreams. I felt I had an eternal connection with the man who wrote 'Hitler. My Part in his Downfall', 'Puckoon' and an assortment of other classics that had reduced me to a state of total rapture upon reading them.

I carefully placed the autograph on a page in my diary at the time, the very same compendium of dark secrets that those two plonkers were to peruse in the interrogation room.

I covered it with a plastic protective film, and it took pride of place in the book. The icing on the cake, for the diary was enormous! My dad had presented it to me in 1981, and it was the biggest journal of its type I had ever seen. The pages were faintly lines, which made it perfect for drawing, and over the next ten years I filled that book with precious items, things that were beyond value. Photos, letters, cartoons, autographs, and bucketloads of writing.

It was my life contained within a book, my legacy, a priceless compendium of irreplaceable treasures, in short, my life's work.

"You should never put all your eggs in one basket, Sid, Kev, Fonz, or Gordon" I hear you say, and you are right.

In the year 2001, my aforementioned annus horribilis, I had lent the book to a pal, who had read it, enjoyed it, and given it back. I collected it from him, put it in the car, and went for a pint. In the pub I met someone whose photo, an early snap of her, featured in the diary. "Oh, I must show you this" I said, and went to the car to retrieve it.

Unbeknownst to me, there were two very shady characters in the pub that day. Members of a notorious crime family from Limerick, whose name I won't mention for reasons of personal safety. The odds of such people being in that pub were astronomical, for it's not that kind of pub, but by some unforeseeable twist of fate they were there at the same time as me, and my precious diary. I later discovered who they were, and that they were out on bail at the time, having been charged with armed robbery, but at the time, I paid them no heed.

That is until one of them asked me "What's the book, man?" to which I answered "It's just my diary man" he picked it up and asked "Is it worth anything, man?" and I, to my eternal regret, said "Just sentimental value, man, unless you count Spike

Milligan's autograph, which might be worth something" he said "Alright man" and went back to the bar.

I then did the daftest thing! I went to the loo, and left the book unattended. When I came out, the two thugs were gone, as was my book. I was a very swift operation too, for I ran outside, and they were already driving away, smiling and waving at me.

The book was gone, and gone forever. After that I didn't write a thing for ten years, my creative juices having been stolen with it. I thought I had reached a sort of perfection with that book that could never be replicated. It was like losing a limb, and when I think of what I lost, I still feel nauseous.

The two geezers were eventually given life sentences, one for murder, and one for a series of rapes in Galway. One subsequently died while working out in the prison gym, but the other, the rapist, is still incarcerated. There is no such thing as bad people, but that's an irrelevance, because we are not talking about people here! The eternal, nagging, question that remains, forever to taunt me, is of course – Does my diary STILL EXIST?

Is it still out there? Do mobsters fight over it as it trundles past their cells on the book cart? "Hey Brookes, man! My turn for Sidney's diary!" Or was it flung from the window of that car as it made its way back to some rat infested ghetto? I shall never know, but it's the not knowing that really hurts.

I wrote many a diary in my day, a fact which, if I remember correctly, is alluded to in the opening lines of this yet to be categorised transcript. They all went missing at one time or other, until I was left with none at all. This includes the one wot I rote in 1980, as a sixteen year old. It was really a testament to lost love, and dealt with my unhealthy obsession with my first infatuation, also previously alluded to. It detailed my adolescent life on a daily basis, which consisted of knocking about on street corners with my pals, hanging out in the pool hall, mitching school and chasing virtuous young Catholic girls to no avail. It was an idealistic time, and the book reflected that. I thought I could solve everything by building a spaceship and bringing a group of young girls of my own choosing to another planet.

That book was missing for almost fifteen years, and then one day, as I sat in the pub, I was approached by a girl from my dim and distant past. "Hey Sid!" she said "My mum found your old diary down the back of our bookshelf!" and she proceeded to hand me the very tome in question, knocking me clear into next week. It was an incredible moment, and re-

reading that book was a real emotional rollercoaster. It is now safely deposited in an antique bureau inherited from my dear old grandmother, along with every other precious item that I still possess.

It amazes me to think of the teenage angst that engulfed me as I wrote that first diary. As sixteen year olds, we really had the weight of the world on our shoulders. There is a passage in the book which recounts a retreat that my class in school undertook. We went to stay for a week in a big country house, forsaking all mod cons and being forced to deal with nothing but the relationships we were having with one and other. It was an incredible rite of passage, and an outstanding memory.

Unrequited love was a common theme throughout the entire group, and after a week it had reduced us all to the brink of suicide. We considered ourselves to be world weary travellers in an unforgiving world. Oh how little we knew! How little we knew!

The Road to Graceland

I believe I was in my early twenties when I went to
visit my mother one day at the house she shared
with my dad in Limerick, and I certainly couldn't
have been much younger than that, as it was shortly
after I had bachelorhood thrust upon me again by
my departing spouse. It was a Saturday, and the
mother was off to do the weekly shopping just as I
arrived. My dad was probably involved in some DIY
project or other, and if that was the case, I was more
than likely trying to avoid being roped in to help. The
upshot was – I decided to join the Ma on her
shopping trip.

We drove into town, and as ever, I spent the next two
hours lagging behind my super fit mom as she went
into shopping overdrive. It was quite an exercise just
trying to stay within view of her as she effortlessly
weaved through the thronging streets. By the end of
it of course, I was knackered, and thinking DIY with
the Da might have been the easier option.

We got back in the car, but there was one more
errand to run, so the Ma said "You stay in the car, I'll
be back in ten minutes" and I readily agreed. She
popped off, and I started fiddling with the car radio. I
got a nice clear reception on one of the channels, and

sat back to listen. When my mum returned, she found her son quite transformed. I was sitting there, wide eyed, dumbstruck and staring blankly into space.

"What's wrong with you now?" demanded my mom. I slowly turned to her and said "It's Elvis Mum. Elvis Presley! I think I get it now." To which my mother replied "Tsk tsk. You're an awful eejit" and promptly drove home. I had had my road to Damascus moment, however, and I was thrust into a state of rapturous delight.

'It's Now or Never' had come on the radio, and the voice of Elvis soared through the car. It hit me like a ton of bricks, it was like a choir of angels had suddenly descended upon that grimy car park. I went from uninitiated to completely converted in the space of three glorious minutes. I suddenly knew what all the fuss was about. Since my childhood, folk, especially my dear cousin Trish, had been raving about this man, but I just didn't get it.

I can safely say that this moment was constituted a sort of emotional rescue, as I was in a very vulnerable place at the time, and from that moment on, I threw myself into a voyage of discovery, listening to every bit of immaculate music ever recorded by his good self. My house quickly became a shrine, and I considered The King to be my saviour. To me, he was the second coming, sent to save the world with rock and roll!

I have regained my senses since, and I realise he was just a man, flawed, like everyone else, but the journey I took back then will never be forgotten, and I can safely say the happiest period of my life took place in 2005, when I sent a week in Memphis with my girlfriend of the time, the inimitable Elizabeth Carver.

We had unlimited access to Graceland, having purchased very expensive VIP tickets, and we actually wandered around that house alone and quite unmolested for hours on end. You always imagine something like that would be anti-climactic, but it surpassed all expectations and then some.

I owe it all to Liz, who arranged the whole thing. For a blessed week of my life, I was very much in love, and in the city of my dreams. Rock and roll utopia. Blues heaven. I can honestly say that the greatest night of my life was spent in BB King's Blues Club on Beale Street. A whole lifetime of dreams packed into one night. My mind was totally blown, every ambition I had ever harboured was realised, and I knew life would never reach such dizzy heights again. Liz will never read this, for she is very far away and determined to stay out of touch, but thanks old girl, from the bottom of my heart.

Mushroom Soup

I met Liz in Durty Nellies, a legendary watering hole
situated just down the road in Bunratty. Durty
Nellies played a significant role in my life, as it was
where I misspent most of my youth. I first had a
drink served to me there at the tender age of
fourteen. Kids today would never believe it, but such
things were a common occurrence back in the day. I
came to inhabit Nellies so much over the years that it
came to inhabit me. Back in those days, the floor
was covered in sawdust, and I knew every separate
wood chip by name. Myself and my young associates
ran amok in there, and in our eyes, we owned the
place. It was all ours. It has the most wonderful old
world atmosphere, having changed very little since it
was founded in 1620. If the pilgrims had just gone to
Nellies instead of sailing off to discover America, they
could have saved us all a lot of bother.
The sense of community that I, and many of the
gangs of which I was an intrinsic part, enjoyed in
Durty Nellies was second to none. Memorable night
after memorable night forged together to form a
perfectly blissful social setting, and we were truly
blessed to be a part of it. Those were the kind of days
that I thought would never end. We became so

entrenched into the very fabric of the place. Its history and atmosphere ran through our veins and we were very much at one with it. An incredible, unbreakable spirit, and a terrific communal vibe.

I had so many profoundly emotional and life changing experiences during my tenure as a resident of the world's greatest pub, and to recount even a fraction of them would be impossible. So many relationships began there, took place there, and ended there. I had my own special seat, down at the back in the corner beside the piano and under the pigeon loft, and there was invariably a seat beside me occupied either by a ravishing female, or an agreeable male friend.

The music was magnificent, it being most famously delivered in our time by Billy, a hoarse, raspy individual who provided wild rebel songs and old Beatles numbers in equal measure, and who never failed to get the blood coursing through your veins. So many long summer evenings, stretching off into infinity, with nothing to do but drink God's good Guinness and enjoy the company of a multitude of likeminded fellow patrons.

Nellies got into my blood. It became a part of the very fibre of my being. I regarded those years as very special. It was a spiritual thing. Those years now occupy a sort of mythic status in my mind. It happened, it happened for many years, and although it sometimes feels as if it happened to someone else, in another country, during a different century, I know for sure that our magical occupation of Nellies is firmly rooted in the annals of local history.

Sadly, I attend far less frequently now. I might pop in for the odd bowl of soup, but everything, with the exception of the pub itself, has now changed beyond recognition. The bricks and mortar remain the same, but the vibe died when the young gangs of Shannon grew up, and we went our separate ways. It is a comfort, however, to know that Nellies is still standing there beside the river, and the man who first served me that pint, when I was fourteen, is still serving pints there, at least he was, the last time I looked.

It was in Durty Nellies, around 1982, that my head first became detached from my body. It was late September, the evenings were becoming considerably shorter, and a mist partially obscured Bunratty Castle, which overlooked our beloved meeting place. Myself and my somewhat bohemian comrades were assembled as usual, inevitably engaged in figuring out our collective finances, as there was a session looming beautifully over the horizon. I was eighteen, already a veteran of many a famous shindig, and I considered myself to be a man of the world.

Now, as it happened, around that time of year, in the surrounding fields, there grew in abundance an interesting fungus called the 'liberty cap'. An inoffensive looking little blighter, it was, to all intents and purposes, a creamy coloured toadstool with a cute bell shaped cap. Magic mushrooms, as they were commonly known, were a part of folklore, and I had always associated them with ancient druids. Legend had it that leprechauns, pixies, fairies and such like, could be seen by someone under the influence of psilocybin, which was the fun guy's active ingredient.

As we sat there that evening, with barely the price of a pint between the lot of us, one member of the company made an announcement. "Hey you guys, have no fear. We shall not need money on this fine evening, for I have been busying myself in the cultivation of an alcohol alternative that will change your life" he said, as he produced an enormous plastic bag from the lining of his jacket. "I have been picking mushies, my dear friends. We shall have a feast."

The contents of the bag were promptly divided equally among us, and we spent the next half hour ingesting them, which was no mean feat, as they were the foulest, most obnoxious tasting, nausea inducing little globules of putrid gunk that you could possibly imagine. But eat them we did, man size helpings of them, and more than a hungry youth could ever need.

There was a chill in the evening, so we adjourned procedures and entered the warmth of Nellies itself. Somebody bought a glass of coke, and our little group assembled around it, all very cosy and together as we made our usual small talk. Half an hour passed, and nothing to speak of took place. The conversation continues, and I had almost forgotten the little feast of an hour previous, when I began to feel a little tingle. Manic giggles had already broken out among a couple of our company, and when this sound became clear to me, the effects of that little feast began to take hold in earnest.

First off, my manically cackling friends developed the features of hideous goblins! They sat there laughing hysterically into my face as they assumed increasingly horrific countenances and began pointing ghastly bony fingers at me, mocking me mercilessly. "Ha ha!! Sidney's coming up! Ha ha! Look at Sidney!" they bellowed, as I tried to shrink into my chair, quite unable to move. These were no longer my friends, they had turned into a group of evil ogres right before my very eyes!

Terrified, I buried my head in my lap and started to stare at the floor. Within seconds, I regretted it as the floor boards started coming apart, and I could clearly see Lucifer and all his clambering minions climbing up ladders towards me. Horrific devils and unutterable creatures from Hell itself were coming to claim me. They were intent of dragging me into Hell, and I could not escape. I lifted my head up, and my friends had transformed into evermore terrifying beings. They were not of this world, and they mocked me without mercy. "Ha ha! Sid's on a bad trip man! Ha ha!"

I looked above their heads, and the ceiling suddenly metamorphosised into an almost exact replica of the Sistine Chapel, with images of God floating about all over the place. God himself began to scorn me, admonishing me with massive gestures that said "To Hell with you. You are not wanted here! Begone! Into the fires of Hell with you!"

At this point, all the background noises inside Durty Nellies gelled together into a giant cacophony, a singular sound which overtook everything. It was geese. An enormous gaggle of geese! I became a goose myself in no time at all! I was a goose, and what's more, I was surrounded by insane, mocking demons! God hates me, and the devil was coming up through the floor to get me. I was rooted to the chair. Movement was impossible as for the next hour I endured this madness. I must have got up somehow, as I found myself outside sometime later. There were tourists mingling with the locals outside, just a typical Nellies evening, but there was something seriously up with me. I had lost my torso! As far as I was concerned, my head was attached directly to my pelvis, my arms were growing out of my hips, and my torso had completely disappeared.

I hid behind a tree, but as small groups walked by, I would walk out and plead with them to help me. "Please help. I can't find my torso. Please help." I begged them, and you can imagine the response I got. I went back behind the tree, and discovered I would levitate at will. My head became totally detached from my pelvis, and it could operate independently. It could float about to its heart's content.

The lads came looking for me then, and they brought me back inside. They had suddenly resumed being themselves, and they seemed to me to be a collection of beatific, saint like creatures. I entered a wonderland, and shared it with my saintly friends for

144

the next nine hours. 'The Mushy Seasons' had begun.

It is true, incidentally, leprechauns, goblins, fairies and suchlike do exist. They are absolutely everywhere. Our ancestors were the first to see them, and under the influence of that innocuous looking hallucinogen, the mushroom, they described them in great detail. They are in the trees. They are in the grass, the sky, the water, absolutely everywhere. They can be seen in precise, unmistakable, clarity, but I for one, will never see them again, as the mushy seasons, of which there were many, have come and gone. They claimed many a victim along the way, and this country is littered with casualties. You don't mess with the brain like that. It's just not smart, and although I would not swap those experiences for anything now, I would not recommend such activity to anyone else. I was lucky to emerge relatively unscathed, and the horrors a chap undergoes, going up, and coming down, are simply not worth it. Having said that, it did instil in me a certain realisation. There is so much more out there than meets the eye. There is a parallel universe full of unimaginable phenomena, and for a brief few years I entered it on a regular basis. I had, of course, gone off the rails long before the onset of that first mushy season, but it cemented my status in the world.

I was a hedonistic headcase intent on self-indulgence at all costs, and my grip on reality slowly unravelled as a consequence. The folly of youth, coupled with a stubborn streak born of my irrepressible O'Sullivan stock, brought about many the situation that I could not control, and I acquired the reputation of a drug-addled directionless young waster, a fecking hippy to be avoided at all costs, and public enemy number one. These commonly held perceptions of your truly were reinforced by a number of unfortunate incidents and I was soon to be smothered in a cloak of infamy.

Myself and a very dear friend were bundled into the cop shop one fateful day, whereupon we were subjected to a humiliating strip search. I microscopic quantity of an incriminating substance was discovered in my shirt pocket. A mere crumb, I assure you, but in those chronically unenlightened times, the possession of a tiny smidgeon of hashish was considered beyond scandalous, and a crime against humanity. My good pal had a wee bit too, and we were duly busted. We were dragged through the courts, and our case made the headlines in The

Clare Champion, a gazette which enjoyed a wide
circulation at the time.

A kindly relative on the O'Sullivan side decided it
would be a good idea to send copies of the offending
article to many other relatives on the O'Sullivan side,
and my reputation within the family became
solidified for all eternity. I guess such things were
considered newsworthy back then. I was, and still
am, entirely immune to such tedious muck raking,
and the opinions of interfering old biddies are of no
consequence to me, but the effect it had on my
parents was unbearable.

I was a thorn in the side of people who loved me
unconditionally, and although I was a headstrong
little git back then, the very idea of making life
difficult for my dear folks, now rankles most
uncomfortably within my soul. Sometime after the
bust, a young local girl took an overdose of her
mother's medication. She got sick, and was
hospitalised. They were pumping her stomach, and a
guard pressed her to reveal the origins of the drugs.
She knew of my reputation due to the newspaper
article, and in an attempt to protect her mother, she
blurted out – "It was Sid! Sid gave me the drugs!"
and the cop received the information gratefully. I

went to the pub shortly after that, and her well meaning dad gave me a bunch of fives! Ouch.

I really had no clue as to what was going on. The young girl was most upset at what she had done, and tried to put things straight, but the damage was done. It reached crisis point shortly after that when I entered the pub again. I was pleasantly surprised to see my dad there, and I approached him for a chat. As I sat beside him, an ignorant cretin emerged from nowhere and began to shout "You gave drugs to my daughter! You bastard! Hanging is too good for ya! You drug dealing bollocks!" I later discovered that this idiot had no daughters, but it was too late, my poor father was mortified, and I would never live it down.

I was eventually cleared of all charges, and managed to ingratiate myself successfully into the community in the following years, but they were dark, dark, times indeed.

Dad

I have not led a blameless life, far from it in fact, but I have suffered the karmic slings and arrows as much as the next man. I have brought my world tumbling down on many occasions through my own crass indifference to actions and their consequences, often taking the wrong course of action when a cleverer alternative was clear. There are events that I cannot mention in this book, and names with which I must exercise the same caution. My reckless actions have caused hurt to many and I haven't always treated people with the respect they deserve. I hope with all my heart those that I have offended can find it in their hearts to forgive me as I enter a new phase in my life.

My dad once took me aside, out of desperation I presume, and we had a little heart to heart. I remember his words thus – "Kevin, I'm going to give you a bit of advice. Disregard everything else you have ever heard, pay heed to these words, and your path through life will be far easier. Be proactive son, and never reactive."

A simple philosophy, but a profound one. From that day on, I have made a conscious effort to give some thought to what I am about to do or say, and I always give due consideration to others, and what they may say or do, before I make up my mind about anything. To stop and think for a second before I act or respond to outside stimulus, and to then actively attempt to respond with something proactive, something positive, and something that never belittles others. A multitude of good things have come from this and although it is not always possible to employ, man being a naturally impulsive animal, it is something that has served me very well.

Wise words from my father, and a clue perhaps to the secret of his success as a man. The ease with which my dad interacted with his fellow man was something to behold. He would mesmerise a room full of strangers, until they felt like lifelong friends. To know him was to have your life enhanced and his natural affinity with people was legendary. He had incredible insight into the human condition, and you would always learn something about yourself after a meeting with him, but he was never patronising and his boundless humour always shone through. I honestly don't know how this world could have functioned without him, as he was such a vital cog in the grand scheme of things.

He was something of a theologian, and he brought something graciously illuminating to spiritual discussions. His plain speaking always led to clear understanding, even for mortals such as myself. Despite his ever practical nature, he had unshiftable faith in something greater than humanity, a creator, if you like. God, by any other name. This confirmed certainty, in fact, always worried me. It led me to believe that my dad knew something that the rest of us didn't, and the more I talked to him, the more convinced of this I became.

There was a charismatic depth to my father that you simply do not find anymore and to simply spend time in his company was a joyous education.

The reader has already guessed, I am sure, that Alexander O'Sullivan is no longer with us. He had many more heart attacks, and the last one of these events, in April 2010, took him from this world. It is a subject I have been struggling to address, but I am glad I have done so, as we must make progress, despite everything. The unthinkable did happen, and he had to tear himself away.

We were inevitably destroyed, but his spirit shines through us, and we are pulling though. I am aware that there are few people extant who could count themselves lucky enough never to have experienced excruciating pain on a par with, or even exceeding, what I felt upon being separated from our dad forever. I don't have to tell such folk how much it hurts for they are now kindred spirits. I was lucky enough to have been in a position to tell my dad how I felt about him, as we discussed his mortality over a pint or two on more than one occasion, and I thought I was well equipped to deal with it.

But nothing prepares you for such a thing. As a family, we helped one and other through it, and we are bonded ever stronger. But it was my dearest and oldest friend who inadvertently helped me to grieve properly. Pascal sent me a text which paid simple tribute to my old man, and the process was complete. It tore me to pieces, which is not as Pascal intended, but I am forever grateful to him for it. The physical hurting ceased and I embraced a renewed acceptance of the life cycle.

The Buddha

Pascal found a receptacle for his seemingly
bottomless well of mental energy in that most
profound of Eastern philosophies; Buddhism. You
might say he has become a leading light in its
movement, embarking on lecture tours throughout
England, and even addressing the House of Lords on
one occasion.

I have dabbled with its concepts myself, and it is a
source of never ending fascination to me, but it takes
a truly expansive mind to grasp it in its entirety.
Through letters and text messages Pascal has shone
a light on the dim areas of my soul, and his
interpretation of death, and the Buddhist viewpoint
itself, are a great comfort. Buddhism does not rely on
fanciful tales of the supernatural to make its point.
IT is merely a way of making sense of the world
around us. It is an attempt to understand ourselves,
and perfectly logical outlook, if you ask me. It
requires great discipline, in that serious study is
required to fully understand it, but its basic concepts
are simple and straightforward.

To paraphrase from one of Pascal's recent messages
"I intend to go deeper in 2013 – Looking at a few
treasures – Service to others – Sincerity and feeling

gratitude for life – Cultivating gems like patience, simplicity and compassion – Your oldest friend – Pascal"

Such things fill my heart with hope and are a never ending source of strength.

Mitching

I attended the graduation ceremony of my son yesterday, and what an occasion it was! Great credit must be given to the University of Limerick, as they really know how to put on a show. My emotions were mixed as I saw my boy make his entrance onto the stage. Pride, predominantly, of course, and a sense of awestruck wonder at our kid's phenomenal achievement. It was never easy, in fact, it was a struggle at times, and to see him finally conferred with his degree was both a relief and a cause for great celebration.

The hall was thronged with the finest examples of young humanity that Ireland has to offer, and to see Shane among them was quite overwhelming. The costumes were fabulous, and I don't think I ever saw so many beautiful people congregated together in one place!

By two o'clock, however, I was back in front of the box, the day being at an end, confronted with he who must surely be the anti-Christ, Noel Edmonds, and other despicable exponents of what passes for afternoon entertainment. It was something of a come-down after the emotional heights of the morning, and I did ponder upon my own shambolic educational history, and the potential which I did piss into the urinals of various manky men's rooms scattered about the land.

"Education is for suckers" we would tell ourselves, my dear friend Brendan and I, as we sat in that fort on freezing December mornings. Resolutely refusing to attend school under any circumstances, we would jump up and down on the spot until lunch time to ward off hypothermia as frost and ice encased our socks and our teeth chattered uncontrollably.

Frozen solid, and covered in pine needles from the predominantly coniferous forests of Tullyglass Hill, I would crawl home for lunch and make very short work of the hot soup and cheese sambos that my dear mum would never fail to have ready.

"How come you're covered with twigs again?" She would enquire, and I would glibly reply "We were on another nature walk, mum" before heading back to the freezing forest where we would have to survive until the end of the school day, when it would be safe to emerge. "This is the best education you can get" we would tell each other. "School does not prepare you for the hardships of life. If we can survive this shit, we can survive anything."

It may not have prepared us for a life within the hallowed halls of academia, but we did survive, and at least I am here to tell the tale. Brendan is not here to read it, however, I am sorry to say. He passed away many years ago, but his spirit is still a powerful presence in my life. Indomitable in life, and in death, that was Brendan Coyne, and although he died far away in India, his legend is forever written in the foundations of Shannon Town.

For it was the *Gangs of Shannon Town* that forged this place. Our generation, and a few previous to it, namely our big brothers and sisters, endlessly pounded the streets in search of something to do, and in doing so, created the character, the history, the soul of our town.

Our gangs lost many a member along the way – Stuffy, Geezer, Cathy, Burch, Johnny, Rob, Gary, Trish, Brendan, the list goes on, but none shall ever be forgotten, and our gangs shall one day unite and come together in a complete celestial group. Those bonds we made shall never be in vain. It all happened for a reason, and the reason for everything will one day be revealed.

I was truly blessed to know the people I knew, the good friends who departed, and the ones who are still with us, but I rarely ever see. The wide ranging and diversified nature of my associations was truly remarkable. I really belonged to something, and

something special belonged to me. It may seem I am
clinging on to a long lost and increasingly vague
concept of togetherness, the principle players having
been flung to every far corner of the Earth, but I feel
the love I developed for my friends shall never
diminish, and I shall nurture it til my dying day,
even if it means wallowing in a puddle of painful
nostalgia forevermore.

My classmates from the Brother's house of horrors,
my squatting comrades from London days, the stable
maids of Worcestershire, my innumerable cousins
from both sides, along with the countless uncles and
aunts, my grandparents (all four of whom I was
lucky enough to share this Earth with), my siblings,
my parents, the girls who broke my heart, the girls I
got my own back on, the thousands of colleagues
with whom I have shared employment, my fellow sad
old gits down at the local turf accountants, Basil and
his assorted friends from the animal kingdom, my
darling nieces – Katy, Shaunagh, Karina, Aisling and
Sarah, Sarah Whitehead, other special friends like
the two Petes and Pascal, dear ones like Angie and
Tom, my formative friends, my footy playing friends,
my drinking buddies, my fellow mitchers, muckers
and messers, my long suffering neighbours during
my Elvis loving heyday, the man that mopped up my

flat, the three blokes who saved me from drowning when I was a kid, my teachers and those that encouraged me in my artistic endeavours, Pontyfax Clan members everywhere, my Applied Physics degree holding son, my endlessly patient employers, Beany who gave me this book, the owner of the shop who caught me nicking *The Beano* when I was a kid, I love you all, unconditionally, and forevermore. There are people who have shone like beacons in my life. People who are so humble that you become humbled by their company. People who are so naturally witty as to leave you with long term damage to the funny bone, spiritually enlightened people whose inner glow is quite blinding, people with the strength to overcome adversity that would leave mortals such as myself floundering, people with talents that leave me dumbfounded, and a multi-faceted mixture of folk who have touched me in so many wonderful ways. It has been an extraordinary odyssey up to this point. Thank you people.

I'd like to thank my producer, Earl Snerbowitz, my makeup lady, Ursula McGillicuddy, without whose help I.. I...

Do give it a rest Sidney!

Do give it a rest.

Ok. Forgive me, 'twas a case of the pen running away with itself. How we started with Shane O'Sullivan's graduation ceremony and ended up with someone called Ursula McGillicuddy is anyone's guess, and I fear that I may be subconsciously prevaricating again as my mind recoils in horror from the prospect of addressing what amounts to a Berlin Wall type structure built across my mind. That which is the nineteen nineties, and following that, what they refer to as the noughties. With this, dear people, we are met with a swirling black hole of impenetrable nothingness.

My existence post 1992 has consisted of working, drinking in my local and sleeping, with the occasional noteworthy even interspersed. The trick now is to try to identify one or two of those events in order to give ourselves something to discuss. I can think of world events, such as the death of Diana, and the September Eleventh atrocity, but I fear I may have wasted my own time in some bizarre experiment.

I may have been trying to create the world's first living robot. An entirely automated being that carries out human functions such as eating, sleeping, shaving and the application of physical gratification through self-appointed methodisation. I think somebody might have been conferred with a degree in just such a thing at the ceremony yesterday, but I digress. The point is, I have existed in a void of my own making for two decades, and I am suddenly faced with pages that I cannot fill. I have brought this about through self-determination, so I cannot complain.

I desperately needed to replace the insecurity I suffered due to my days spent as a footloose vagabond with something altogether more predictable, I needed a life where nothing out of the ordinary happened, and I fear I have succeeded beyond my wildest dreams.

While I have been comfortably numb, of course, events have taken place around me. My son, who was two in 1992, is now twenty two, and any day I spent in his company during the past twenty years, as I watched him grow up, was a day spent in exceptional circumstances, where the robot was in human mode, and had a reason for being. That was certainly time well spent, and there was a certain symbolic validation of this auto-man's valiant attempts at fatherhood on display at the University yesterday. It has to be said, however, that all work in that respect was carried out with the full cooperation of Shane himself, and he really made it quite easy for me.

As antiquity entered my bones, drinking became increasingly difficult. I drank on a Friday evening, and over time, I began to find that I became tired and emotional as a result. A week's work was no longer the ideal preparation for a session, and I found myself getting pretty sick of it. I started to find it difficult to relate to anyone on any sort of level while engaged in the gargle ritual, and it became perfunctory. It was the drinking robot's obligation to the ghost of the formerly social Sidney to attend to drunken responsibilities, such as murdering Elvis songs and stewing in perpetual misery.

I enjoyed a sense of well-being for a few precious hours on a Saturday, with a few pals around, some footy on the telly and a game of pool in progress, but that feeling would soon pass, and the futility of what amounted to self-harm became glaringly apparent. Drinking was confined to Fridays and Saturdays, but it was still a defining theme, and the week was spent in recovery. I didn't even qualify as a proper alcoholic, but I knew it was time to stop. I can't of course, explain away two decades by claiming they went by in a sort of black-out, I just became such a creature of routine, that drinking was supposed to provide a social break in that routine, but I derived nothing positive of a social nature from it, and eventually the break in the routine was the routine, and I was in total auto-pilot between piss ups!

There was great camaraderie in my local, a Drumgeely institution on stilts called The Crossroads Tavern. I was never more at home anywhere, and its patrons to this day are the salt of the Earth. I miss them, but needs must, and my will to survive, and to consign hangovers to history, far outweighs any desire I might have to continue searching for answers at the bottom of a pint glass.

Swimming

The one concession I made to a healthier lifestyle during those years was swimming. While submerged in water, the body and mind feel no pain, for some miraculous reason, and coupled with a stint in the steam room, the Saturday morning swim was an effective hangover therapy. That is, of course, while you were still undertaking the treatment. Once the swim was finished, and you were back out in the fresh air, the sickness would kick in for real, and the only cure known to man was more drink.

When we were very young, and still resident in Crawley, Sussex, our parents would often deposit us at the local swimming pool, where on a Saturday, you could swim all day for the princely sum of one penny. I teamed up with Cousin Trish on such days, and we were inseparable. You could not prise us apart, and I'm sure she won't mind me confessing to the fact that we were the original kissing cousins! We did, however, quickly become separated once we entered the water, as Trish was two parts human and three parts fish! She was the original girl from Atlantis, and had webbed feet to prove it. I kid you not, her toes were actually gelled together and she went through the water like a knife through butter.

The girl was a water baby, and that was that! She made it look so easy, but of course it wasn't, as I was to find out to my cost one fine summer's day in 1970.

I would cling onto the bar and watch in awe as Trish the fish zipped up and down at an incredible rate of knots, but I never went to the deep end, as it was strictly forbidden for little non-swimmers such as myself. But as the weeks went by, I would inch a little closer to the forbidden zone, hoping no one would notice. They didn't notice and I eventually found myself clinging to the bar right smack in the middle of the deep end! All seven foot deep of it, what a thrill! I was such a big boy now! Hanging out with all the adults!

Just then, someone else showed up, and they too were holding onto the bar. What's more, they needed to get past. So without thinking, I let go of the bar, let them past, and grabbed hold of the bar again. For all of five seconds I had floated in the deep end without needing the bar! Now, what a terrible little gobshite I must have been, for having completed this manoeuvre, I instantly became convinced that I could swim!

"It's easy!" I thought "I just did it" and you guessed it, I promptly propelled myself right out into the middle of the pool with a big powerful kick of my lanky little legs. I screamed and thrashed about for a second or two, upon realising that I could not swim and started to sink to the bottom.

I remember it so well, it is like yesterday. I was floating about under water, everything was muffled, and I was beginning to feel all woozy, but strangely contented.

Just then, I was hit with an almighty thud by something akin to a marine bulldozer. Bang! It hit me, and then, bang! and biff! Again, like a sub aqua episode of *Batman*. I literally flew up out of the water and onto the side of the pool.

Something very violent had occurred. I had been attacked by sea monsters, I thought, but I had in fact been saved from drowning by three blokes who who now stood towering over me at the poolside, shaking their heads in admonishment. I was bruised all over from my underwater bashing and I stumbled to my feet and walked off. I didn't even thank the swimmers. As far as I was concerned there had been no call for them to get that rough!

I had survived a near death experience, but all I could think about was getting dressed and going into Crawley Town. It was time to stand outside the telly shop in the hope of spotting Georgie Best again.

Miss you, Trish.

Brothers Revisited

Mr Kennedy's car broke down one day, and for a while, I was forced to walk the six miles to school with the Unchristian Brothers. The walk was fraught with danger in my eyes, and I had all sorts of obstacles to negotiate. The bag weighed a ton, and the strap threatened to amputate my arm from the shoulder down. Many Irish kids can relate to that, I know, but as far as I was concerned, I had been specifically singled out for unspeakably horrific punishment.

I took advantage of the walk to recite times tables and bewildering Irish grammar.

"Six times six is forty, seven times six is forty seven, bhí mé, tá mé, an bhuil tu dul amach?" I would mutter, as the spectre of the school loomed larger and larger on the horizon. One morning, while wrapped up in my recitations, and in a state of fearful distraction, I started to cross the last road before the point of no return. Half way across, I was sent flying into space by the bonnet of a homemade car belonging to one of the brothers!

I had been knocked down within a foot of the school gates! It was a homemade car, and only capable of travelling at around five miles per hour, but it was serious enough for the brother to drive me home. I had a huge bruise on my leg, and I nurtured it for a week, praying that it would never diminish. But I did recover, and it was off to school again.

I cursed that brother, though he wasn't the worst of them. He wasn't one of the leather bearing happy slappers, he was a rather mild mannered man in fact. No. I cursed him because he hadn't killed me. Could he not have been driving a nice big car at 90 mile an hour? Or better still, a Sherman tank?

Even the desks we sat at were straight out of the dark ages, replete with ancient bone ivory inkwells. I would sit and wonder about a long line of traumatised predecessors, unable to stare out of the blackened windows and dreading their turn to recite the times tables, as the leather was warmed up on the hands of some other unfortunate wretch. I suppose I had a taste of what it was like for my forefathers in some of the less savoury educational institutions of Ireland, and I was present at a transitional period in our history, being among the last of a generation of corporal punishment victims, and in a peculiar sort of way, I am almost grateful for that.

They certainly toughened up that weedy little English boy, and that in itself was a vital preparation for some of the scrapes I'd get into in later life.

Squat Rot

I was in possession of a fairly well-appointed squat
once. I think it may have been in Willesden, close to
my old pal Geezer, who I believe was domiciled with
his girlfriend across the road. It was a spacious
apartment, with all the mod cons and convenient
access to all the local amenities, principally the Royal
Oak Pub, which served a passable pint of Guinness,
all things considered.

I lived alone in this squat for whatever reason, and it
was very homely indeed. I used to visit pals in
Brighton on occasion, and did so one weekend,
whereupon I had a marvellous time. It was party
central, and the craic was mighty! Brighton was
another one of those towns that a chap just feels a
natural affinity with.

I was all parties out as I made my way back to
London, and I was looking forward to a week's
recuperation back at the squat. Much to my
surprise, however, when I entered the landing, I
discovered things were not quite as I had left them!
There seemed to be at least forty coats scattered
about and a rising crescendo of noise greeted me as I
approached he door of the front room.

"Could be some of the lads come to visit" I thought, as I opened the door, but the moment I did, a sudden silence descended on the proceedings, and I was greeted by a most unexpected vista.

There, staring with equal surprise back at me, was a large group of gentlemen that I had never seen before, all gathered around the coffee table, which was decorated with many a bottle of beer, and quite a number of whiskey bottles to boot. There was a deathly silence for at least a minute, until I managed to meekly squeak "Er... Hello... Wot's you lot doin' 'ere then? This is my gaff."

They began to mumble incoherently to one and other for a while, until this enormous mountain man with a huge ten gallon hat and a ton of jewellery around his neck stood up and said "Hello to you sir. We are sorry to intrude, I am Chief Christy O'Connor. These are my people. We have arrived today from Kerry, that's in Ireland, sir, and this is our new home." Or words to that effect. I wasn't in a position to argue, and I said "Well, there's plenty of room for everybody, so long as I get my bedroom, you're all welcome." This was greeted with warm mumblings, none of which I could fathom, as there appeared to be an unfamiliar dialect being utilised, but the consensus seemed to be agreeable.

Christy and his tribe of Kerrymen immediately assumed I was English due to my accent, and no amount of counterargument on my part would convince them otherwise. The older ones among them, your stereotypical Irish émigré with cloth cap and confirmation suit circa 1947, milled about me, shook my hand and thanked me for my kindness. They couldn't quite believe that this English man had allowed them all to stay so readily, and they quickly furnished me with a powerful tipple or two, and I sat into the session for a while, before retiring to my bed.

We shared the squat for a few weeks, and things went smoothly enough. On occasions some of the younger bogmen would fight each other, and you often find them lying about the place half battered to death, but I got used to it. The big chief, Christy, kept them under control for the most part. He was a very authoritative man and he seemed to be in charge of the communal finances, supplying endless booze to his tribesmen, and bringing in the occasional basket of bread and cheese, which appeared to complete this motley crew's dietary needs.

I was treated with deference as 'The Landlord' for the most part. I grew to like some of the older gents very much, and a happy medium was reached. Then, one night, I went over to visit Geezer in his squat across the road. It was a typical evening, being treated to Geezer's unique viewpoint on the world, and being party to his even more unique guitar playing. Geezer was a great musician, like so many of my friends, and he had an amazing ability to pluck obscure songs, unknown, it seemed, to anyone else but him, right out of the air, and play them perfectly. We drank a little, and partook of a doobie or two. Fun times with Geezer, who now entertains other departed souls in that place that we like to call Heaven.

I had a fierce dose of the munchies as I headed back to the squat. These were lean times, however, and I hadn't got two shillings to rub together. I got in, and the usual session was underway in the front room, singing and fighting in equal measure. I had no food of my own, as my giro had not arrived that week, but I decided to take a chance and raid the fridge. I helped myself to a cheese sandwich and went to bed, to dream of Irish nymphettes and frolics in the fields with Basil, no doubt.

I was vaguely aware of birds singing when I awoke, which made it seem unusually early in my mind, but as I opened my eyes I became of something much more alarming. I could feel something sharp pressing against my throat! I thought I must be dreaming, but then I heard myself gurgling and was wide awake in an instant.

I saw a huge frame, replete with gigantic hat, looming in front of me, and it soon became clear that the chieftain, none other than Christy himself, was holding a knife under my chin.

"Good morning, Landlord!" he screamed, and frothing at the mouth, he continued "You like cheese, do you, Landlord? You would leave a man without his breakfast, would you? Give me one reason why I should not kill you, Landlord, as I have killed many men before you for less!"

He pushed his face right into mine, and I could not even so much as swallow, for fear of having my neck torn asunder. His breath made me want to retch, but I was frozen solid in fear. This lunatic was almost certainly going to kill me for stealing his cheese. In time, he eased the pressure and bellowed "Speak Landlord! Or forever hold your peace!" and I whimpered – "Fuck! Please don't kill me, Chief! I'll give you anything, all the cheese you can eat! Anything! Don't kill me! Please!" To this, the Chief replied "What about the room, Landlord? I like the

room. Can I have the room?" and I readily replied
"Wot? The room? Yeah. Take it, it's yours!"
We agreed that I would not be around when he
returned that day with fresh cheese, and sure
enough, I never did see the chief again. I went in
search of another squat, and found some grotty hole,
but it was a damn sight better than being dead.
I did not drown in the Crawley baths, the homemade
car had insufficient force, and I survived my
encounter with a deranged chief who had been
deprived of his cheese. I have been spared,
mercifully, on three occasions. But why? Does
someone want me to write this book? And if so, what
happens if and when I finish it? Will the shock kill
me? Or will I slowly expire from separation anxiety?

Tight spots indeed, I've been in a few. But I have led a relatively quiet life since the end of the eighties. Attempting to pen this memoir has in fact brought home the extent to which I am presently existing in a state of self-imposed inertia. No news is good news, mind you, as they say, and I suppose reaching what is, to all intents and purposes, middle age, is a huge contributing factor. I should count myself fortunate to be enjoying such an uncomplicated existence. I have strived to reach this point, and although it could not be considered a high point by any means, it is a point of astronomically elevated proportions when compared to some of the depths to which I have fallen.

I should have strode through life with unbridled confidence, big strapping lad that I am, but my demeanour was always blighted by a niggling unease. This niggling unease would sometimes give birth to an all-consuming sense of insecurity, which in turn would lead to all sorts of anxiety. Reaching middle age, or thereabouts, in a relatively unscathed condition and with some provision made for the future, is nothing short of miraculous, and difficult though it may be, I remind myself of those low points in an attempt to instil within myself some sense of personal achievement, however fragile, or however tenuous that may be. You ate ice lollies out of bins, Sidney Pontyfax; you ate ice lollies out of bins!

Indeed and I did, thank you very much, and it could not be considered a fulfilling moment (nor a sufficiently filling one), even if I did harbour an ambition to be a tramp when I was a boy. That was a moment far removed from the glamour my young mind attached to the lot of a roving vagabond, and no mistake. I realised then that being a tramp wasn't all about wide open spaces, sleeping under the stars and availing of apple pie and sexual favours from buxom housewives.

No, indeed. It was more about being in a state of frantic uncertainty regarding just about everything. Your next meal, your next bed, the next time you are going to get a chance to wash yourself, and whether or not any of these things are ever going to come your way again.

I was a tramp for a day, on the seedy streets of London, and I was reduced to eating a half melted ice lolly which I retrieved from a bin before a Scotsman called Colin Stewart Cambell saved my worthless little life.

I had worked for a while in Dickensian sweat shop, deburring excess plastic from bottle tops for twelve hours a day while standing rigid til rigor mortis set in. I had had quite enough and I left of my own accord. But under the rules of the social welfare, I was not supposed to willingly leave a position of employment, and when I went to claim some benefit they said all payment would be suspended for six weeks. The stony faced so-and-so would not give me a supplementary and sent me back out into the world stony feckin' broke, so she did! It took hours to walk back to the squat, and when I arrived, I found to my horror that it had been boarded up. They put a ghastly contraption called a spider lock on the front door, from which they did hang the dreaded repossession order.

I was in a right pickle, and I had been wandering around for hours in a zombielike condition, starving my arse off, when I met Colin Stewart Cambell, the Scotsman. I had met him briefly some time before that in one of London's desolate drinking dives, The White Horse, Harlesden.

"Hoots, Sid, mon, how goes it?" he asked, and I told him the whole sorry tale. He didn't have much himself, but he took me straight to the greasy spoon for the best meal I ever had. Omelette, chips and beans! He put me up, and fed me for as long as it took. The man was a veritable saint. Blessings be upon you, Colin Stewart Cambell.

I often wonder what became of Colin Stewart Cambell, who insisted on being addressed by his full title, by the way. I kept a little diary detailing our adventures together during that short period. He loved it, and was very creatively encouraging. I gave him that little book. Perhaps he still has it. He took me under his wing, and he didn't have to do that. The world is full of selfless people like him, but they generally keep to themselves, having no need to advertise. I was just lucky to bump into one at my lowest point, but I've always been lucky when it comes to the really essential things, I guess.

Footy

I know I have been waffling on about myself for ages
now, and it borders on egotistic narcissism, and
that's a bit of a mouthful, as the actress said to the
bishop, but it is a sort of a memoir we have going
here, and I challenge anyone to write such a thing
without overly employing the dreaded letter I. The
word memoir also makes me a little uncomfortable
as I feel a tad underqualified. I have yet to do
anything that has attracted the attention of the
world, after all. But perhaps I will go down in history
as the first man to write a memoir based on a
seemingly uneventful life. So, with your kind
forbearance, and in the hope that you will not
consider me an ego-centric, self-indulgent twit with
an English accent, I will continue to trawl through
that barren wasteland of non-events, my memory.
Inevitably, when I start scouring those battered old
memory banks, my mind tends to alight on the
boiler, Tola Park, circa 1978. I guess it's just a nice
comforting place to be. Long summer nights
stretching into infinity with nothing to do but obsess
about football and girls. For adolescents such as
myself and Pascal, these were very serious subjects
indeed.

Powered by endless bowls of cornflakes, we would
spend the first two thirds of every day partaking in
footy matches that involved most of the other local
lads. Great rivalries were formed on that little pitch
in Tola Park. A pitch that was like Wembley Stadium
to us, with plenty of room for Pascal to weave his
magic. I still walk past it frequently, and it looks like
a cabbage patch that you could barely swing a cat
on, but that matters not, for to us, during those
magnificent long summers, it was an expanse of
pristine green land on which we could all act out our
footy fantasies, being wing wizards, dominant
captains, midfield maestros and goalkeepers who
regularly defied the laws of physics while carrying
out unfeasibly superb saves.

How we loved to play, and we would do so every day
til dusk. I was a trifle laborious when I played
outfield, despite imagining myself to be on par with
Glen Hoddle, but I was fairly handy between the
sticks, and I often harboured ambitions in that
regard. My dad was a great goalie in his day, and he
was on the books with Shelbourne FC, a top Dublin
club. I'd like to say I took after him, and perhaps I
did, to an extent, but my great downfall was nerves.
I tried out for a team in Dublin once, and I was so
terrified that I froze completely solid while the

practice match went on around me. I made a couple of attempts to get involved and ended up looking a total gobeen. I played on infamous game for a team which comprised players from my dad's company and Mick Ring's company. It was an inter-firm match, and in my mind, it was a huge deal because my dad, Mick, and loads of my contemporaries would be in attendance, all dying to see Sid the famous goalie kid making his big debut.

First, they gave me a kit that was ten times too small, so I could not move my arms freely, and secondly, there was a huge pothole in the goalmouth, which I seemed to fall into every time the ball came anywhere near me. I let in about seven goals, over my head as I stepped back into the hole, under my legs, and in the most embarrassing ways known to man. I was unmercifully pilloried from the sideline, and they never asked me to play again. It was traumatic, and so unfair, because in my head I was still that agile little kid making impossible saves to rapturous applause from Pascal and the boys of Tola Park.

A very short-lived football career, but over the years I was still lucky enough to be a part of a great street soccer culture, Shannon style. I played with some legends of the game. People like Mick Callahan and

Ian Burchill, who along with Pascal, could have played professionally in their sleep, and come to think of it, probably did!

Footy is a wonderful in my eyes, and it formed a huge part of our lives. It bonded me with my father to a great extent, so much so, that after he passed I found it difficult to take an interest in the beautiful game for a while. My fanaticism soon returned, but it shall never really be the same. I still look at my phone during a televised match expecting to receive a comment from Pops. Something along the lines of "He's got his shooting boots on today!" or "That goalie needs to rethink his vocation." As some poor hapless fool lets the ball trickle between his legs.

It's the great unifier, footy. That poor hapless fool, though he be a highly paid professional, is on the same level as the rest of us as he despairingly flaps about. Just as watching Lionel Messi mesmerising opponents today puts me in mind of Pascal running rings around the rest of us when we were kids.

It is a simple thing. A spherical leather object pumped up with air, a flat surface, some jumpers for goalposts and you are up and away!

In 1986, I remember, I flew into Shannon for what was ostensibly a short holiday, I hung about in Nellies with my dear friends Mandy and Murph for a couple of weeks and had the time of my life. Just to breathe Irish air after the smut of London Town was an unimaginable treat, and I revelled in it for all it was worth.

I was staying with my folks on the hill, of course, and life was good. Then the question of how long my holiday in Ireland was going to last came up. "Do you have any plans, Kevin?" was the pressing enquiry from the direction of my somewhat exasperated folks. "I'm not going anywhere until after the World Cup!" was my resounding reply, and I stayed stuck under their feet until it started a few weeks later.

I am really glad I did, now, as '86 was when a certain Diego Maradona won the damn thing almost singlehandedly, and watching it with my dad now forms one of the greatest memories I have. Being a stubborn, unscrupulous little fecker really paid off that summer, but I had to haul my carcass back on to the road, and I did so reluctantly. This time around it was so hard to say by bye to Basil, the folks, and Ireland's green pastures, but luckily for me, I was destined to fart about in London for only a blessedly short time before returning. Galway beckoned, and myself and Basil would enjoy some of our greatest adventures together.

Just as was the case years before in Shannon, myself and my faithful hound would become a familiar sight on the streets of that tribal city. We were up against its unforgiving elements, relentless icy cold rain and a wind that would cut right through ya, and times were so hard that I was often tempted to pilfer some of my best pal's pedigree chum, but were in it together, just the two of us against the world, and we were happy.

The Pontyfax Clan

Since my early teens, I have enjoyed the exalted position of leader of the world's most celebrated organisation.

A collection of wonderful folk, including Sue, Fred, Samantha, and the most recent recruit – Pontyfax Junior.

We are the Pontyfax Clan.

Our star may have dimmed since our inception in the late seventies, but upon circulation of this missal, I am expecting a significant re-ignition of interest. It's easy to join. All you need to do is pick a Pontyfax name for yourself. So, if, for example, your name is Ignatius Moriarty, all you need to do is pick a new forename for yourself, like let's say, Cedric, and hey presto! You are now Cedric Pontyfax.

Thereafter, you are required to absolutely nothing. The Pontyfax

Clan has no belief system, and members are not expected to adhere to a doctrine of any description. We do nothing, and as your leader, I too, do nothing. It's win win, all the way. There is no fee, and it is left to the discretion of female members as to whether or not they wish to engage in physical activity with their beloved leader (I would suggest a game of table tennis for those that feel that way inclined.)

The creation of the clan was an idle, frivolous and ultimately pointless thing to do, and that is precisely the point. The employment of passive nihilism is essential! The Pontyfax Clan calls for a re-evaluation of all values, but at the same time, it doesn't, because it can't be bothered. Ask for nothing, and you shall receive nothing, and nothing is the very concept that we seek to embrace. Mankind's most dangerous enemy is clutter, we must make an effort to de-clutter.

We must dispense with the fruitless pursuit of understanding and embrace absolute nothingness. Anybody wishing to do nothing about it is welcome to join the Pontyfax Clan, and those that don't bother have already joined through inaction.

So it's win win all the way, unless you prefer to lose, which is perfectly acceptable too.

That is exactly the sort of nonsense I would have written in my 1980 diary, when I was prone to a sort of anti-idealistic idealism and I wanted to run off to Mars with a select group of delectable females. I appear to be regressing, but I can say that almost all of my beliefs have come full circle since my cult leader days, and I am now instilled with an absolute certainty that the non-principles espoused by myself and my ragged band of non-followers were ill conceived, counterproductive and blatantly incorrect. There is more to the human condition than humans will ever comprehend, and the pursuit of a state of nothingness is a criminal waste of mental resources. Still, it was popular in its day, and fun while it lasted.

I was the notorious bandit Sid the Kid back then, and I emblazoned my name throughout the town with my weapon of choice – the trustworthy magic marker. It was my mission to inscribe "Sid the Kid wos 'ere" upon every inch of space available to me, and pretty soon I was a household name.

I was that damned elusive vandal, Sid the Kid leader of that infamous band of outlaws, the Pontyfax Clan, and a youth of renowned intemperance.

You were likely to see my name in the most unlikely places. On the back of the bench in front of you as you attended church, daubed into the much of the wing of a police car, on the back of cereal boxes in the supermarket, on the walls of the ladies toilets, on every lamppost in town without exception, on busses and trains, and on every single item of school equipment in St. Patrick's Comprehensive.

189

That is until one day, when I was actually attending
school for once, and we were involved in a 'games'
session. 'Games' sessions in those days consisted for
a run around the country with our P.E. teacher at
the time, an agreeable gentleman called Mr. Tuomey.
Now long distance running was never our thing, so at
the first opportunity myself and my pals would run
for cover. We would stand under a tree and smoke
butts until the runners came back our way again,
whereupon we would walk back to class. This
defeated the purpose of the exercise, of course, but
that's another story.

One such day, as we were huddled together under a
tree, coughing and wheezing, we were approached by
a girl who possessed the brightest, sunniest smile on
God's green Earth. It was none other than Cathy
Doolin, and she had some news for me.

"Mister Garvey is looking for you, Kev. He seems
really mad." She said, as I stood under the tree,
nonchalantly drawing on my gold bond, pretending
to be cool, and trying not to betray my pent up
feelings of absolute adoration for Cathy. "Oh. Ta,
Cath. I shall see him in my office forthwith." I said,
as I was slowly being invaded with trepiditious dread.
The runners came around again, and from behind
the tree, we jumped back into their midst,

undetected, and trotted a little, before pretending to be knackered and walking back to the school building.

No sooner had I walked in the door, but from behind me came the booming voice of a very agitated Mr Garvey. "ARE YOU SID THE KID?" he shrieked, turning my blood cold on the spot. He repeated his enquiry, quite forcibly, again and again and his voice reached an inhuman pitch as he did so, until I was forced into a full confession. I was indeed, Sid the Kid, and I knew in my heart that I was in for it! Mr Garvey frogmarched me around the school, pointing out my offending handiwork around every turn. On walls, desks, chairs, windows, blackboards, dusters, library books, floors, ceilings, you name it, Sid the Kid "wos there" in all his glory.

"What are you going to do about it, Sid the Kid?" demanded Mr Garvey. I was thinking I could change my name, but I thought I had better not suggest that particular course of action. "I could clean it up" I meekly responded, instead. Mr Garvey kindly supplied me with a cloth and some detergent, and I set to work. I was required to clean every inch of the school, and it took aeons.

The saddest moment came about in the toilet when I across what to me was an item of historic importance. There, on the inside of the door, in very faint lettering was "Jon. Leeds United 1972" and It was with a tear in my eye that I was forced to wash it away. Bremner, Lorimer, Eddie and Frenky Gray, Johnny Giles, all the greats of that fantastic team would be forgotten forever.

It was abject mortification at the time, but it was an episode that featured my dear friend Cathy, who is no longer with us, and for that reason it is a very precious memory. In later life, she worked in the local chemist, and I was frequently treated to that smile. It was a smile that was to form part of the traditional fabric of our town. I have lost many family members and dear friends, but I have always managed to come to terms with it. With Cathy, I still find it impossible to accept, and I know I never will. I know she has only gone from this world, but we need some light in this world too.

I had an American friend called Ken once. He was going out with the venerable Valerie Driscoll and the three of us were sharing a cosy little homestead in London with some other memorable folk. I don't know how it came about, but I found myself working in the Albert Hall with Ken on one occasion. We were part of a catering crew that must have been desperate for bodies, as we were hired on the spot, no questions asked. There were some kind of posh indoor tennis tournament going on and it was our job to wait on all these tuxedo clad gentlemen and their jewellery rattling partners.

Myself and Ken had a rare old time doing this, and we were knocking back leftover tipple all night. We got quite sozzled in fact. Expensive champagne and caviar, don't you know. The posh folk went home, and we were left to clear up, whereupon we got slightly more inebriated on what they had left behind.

We were there all night, wandering around one of London's most famous landmarks to our heart's content and without interference from anybody. They really should have done a security check on me, for I was Sid the Kid, the well-known magic marker man. I came across a beautiful painting on one of the walls. It was a depiction of the Queen and her sister when they were little nippers. I would say this thing was worth a pretty penny or two. If you ever come across it, look carefully at the bottom left hand corner. There you will see that the artist went under the most unusual of names. Is Sid the Kid really an appropriate title for a court appointed portrait painter?

I should think not.

A Close Encounter with Madonna's Bra

I remember going in search of a new squat one day
with my friend and partner in crime at the time, one
Mr Martin Lyons. We were more like a comedy
double act with me playing the straight man for
once, and things often got out of hand, to say the
least, instability being the pervasive order of the day,
but we looked out for each other, and that was what
it was all about.

It was late on a Friday evening when myself and the
bold Martin finally came across what seemed to be a
suitable abode. A nice little two bedroomed flat on
the ground floor of a fairly upmarket block in
Willesden. We gained entry quite easily through an
open window and were busily giving the place a once
over with a dustpan and brush when we had some
unwelcome visitors. It seemed that some local
busybody had objected to our presence there, and
the Old Bill suddenly appeared on our new doorstep.
"Get in the van, gents. You're nicked." Was the order
issued, and we had little choice but to comply.

In the back of the van, with Martin freaking out a
little, I asked the coppers why we were being
arrested. "Suspicion of breaking and entry, mate."
Was the cursory response. "But we didn't break in,

your honour" I protested "The window was open."

"No skin off our noses, Paddy" says he, and I knew there was no point in arguing.

They drove us to Willesden green nick, checked us in, and consigned us to separate cells until the next gathering of magistrates at the local courthouse, which, much to our horror, was to be the following Monday. My cell was a dank, dark, dreary concrete box with a bucket in the corner and a dripping tap. Yep, just like in the movies!

After a couple of hours, they threw another bloke in with me. He was an Englishman who had been nicked for drunk driving, and he proceeded to whine about the "facking injustice" of his situation for hours on end, demanding a solicitor and some "facking edible grub, you bastids" until he had me driven half demented.

I calmed him down after a while with some conciliatory chatter, and he went to sleep. I saw the same bloke a few months later in the Royal Oak, but when I approached him to say hello, he said "fack off, Paddy" and carried on drinking his ale. Some people, huh?

Come that night, Saturday night and Sunday night, the entire cell complex was turned into a heaving drunk tank. Packed to the rafter with predominantly

Irish pissheads, all singing and telling bawdy jokes. There were a few thrown into my cell, and it turned out I knew them! A bunch of cracking lads from a village near Shannon. We had a good old laugh that night, despite the circumstances.

The food sucked, and being a veggie did not help, but I was a hardy enough individual back then, and I survived until Monday morning. I was more concerned about a job I had just landed, than anything else. I had answered an ad looking for photographers at Wembley Stadium and much to my astonishment, I had been accepted, and was to start training at 2pm that day, at the stadium itself. Needless to say, myself and Martin were in quite an unwashed state when we were reunited at the courthouse.

When our case came before the assembled beaks, one of the arresting officers stood up and said "The defendants were cooperative throughout, and Mr O'Sullivan has informed us that he is to start work as a photographer at Wembley Stadium today, if it pleases the bench" which was very decent of him, I thought, and the magistrates let us off with a warning. We were determined to keep our squat, and we went straight back to it. We had left the door open, and calmly reclaimed it, cocking a hoop to any interested onlookers in the process.

I got cleaned up, had some of Martin's famous cheese sandwiches á la garlic, and headed for Wembley.

A woman called Rosie met me there and took me to her office. Inside the office was a bunch of polaroid cameras and a collection of cardboard cut-outs. Much to my delight, I found myself in a room full of Madonnas!

Rosie gave me a camera, a cut-out, and instructions to photograph punters standing beside the image of the singer as they arrived for that evening's concert. I would also get free access to that concert, and the next two! Both at Wembley! Wow! How cool was that! I readily accepted the job, and although the public were entirely disinterested in purchasing a photo from me (I sold one) I had a lot of fun outside with my life size model of Madonna.

I was also given free reign of Wembley and explored the place extensively. That's when I found myself outside Madonna's dressing room. I just stood there as people flew about outside the room in a panic, running in and out with different costumes and suchlike. I didn't see her, but I could hear her giving out stink inside. There was a wardrobe just outside the door full of conical bras and suchlike. I absent mindedly put my hand out, and had just touched one of the great Madonna's bras when someone wheeled the wardrobe away.

I touched Madonna's bra!

I don't know how many people can say that, now that I think of it, there are probably quite a few, but that was quite a weekend, eh, Martin, me old mucker?

Rare Ol' Times

How often have you gotten on a plane only to have
your journey blighted by some screaming kid in the
aisle opposite? Does it seem as if you are continually
accompanied on your travels by that same yelling,
whining little wretch, or someone of his or her ilk?
Yep. I know that feeling. But I am here to tell you
that in future you should have some sympathy, and
show a little compassion for the little mite, because
that unfortunate creature was once me!

The first time I flew on a plane, my wild excitement
at the prospect was soon replaced with unbearable
agony as the cabin pressure caused my infant brain
to explode! Nothing could console me once the
damage was done, and I bawled my eyes out for the
entire duration. In fact, I may have given my relatives
the impression that I was a whimpering little English
softy when we arrived in Dublin.

When we were young, and still resident in England,
we would make the occasional trip to the homeland
of my parents. To be precise, Carnlough Road, Cabra
West, Dublin, the very street on which they both
grew up, and on which, as youngsters, they courted.
We would usually get the boat, but on this occasion
it was a plane, and my head was still reverberating

with the agonised echoes of my ordeal when we arrived at my granny's, no doubt causing my relatives to enquire "What's wrong with that snotty little fecker?" as I wobbled about in the kitchen, quite unable to get my bearings.

Culture shock does not begin to sum it up. Baptism of fire does not get close. For us, as children, travelling to Dublin was akin to arriving in the outer reaches of the planet Neptune. After the sedate avenues of suburban Sussex, Cabra West was another world entirely. It was immediately head expanding as my horizons opened up to reveal my extended family. Huge swathes of cousins milled about, much to my delight, as I was suddenly presented with endless opportunities to get up to all sorts of mischief.

My Dad had nine siblings, who were, scattered about the place, though quite a few remained in Dublin and we would often descend on my mother's folks, Paddy and Sarah Brennan, in Cabra. Countless cousins would fly about that house on any given Sunday as my old Gran struggled to keep control with desperate pleadings to Jesus Christ our saviour. In fact, when I was a kid, I thought dear old Granny Brennan's vocabulary was confined to three often repeated phrases. "Jesus, Mary and holy Saint

Joseph", "Sacred heart of Jesus" and "Saints
between us and all harm". She was a great old
character, and a real throwback to tougher times,
when you hadn't a bean to feed your family with and
deranged dentists would gleefully pull all your teeth
with a rusty old pliers as you wriggled around
praying for the invention of anaesthesia.

Paddy Brennan was a beautiful, soft hearted old
man, fond of his pint and a sing song, with an ever
present, half smoked, player's senior service tucked
behind his ear. A true Dub, through and though.

My Mom had eight siblings of her own, and they were
almost always in attendance on a Sunday. I
worshipped my uncles, Noel, John, Martin, Gerry
and Paddy, and I spent many blissful hours of sleep
snuggled up in a bed with large numbers of them
until the beloved household mutt, Major, would come
calling in the morning, lick us and half to death and
send the uncles off to work "on the buildings" with
my dear grandad.

They all likes to play footy, and I guess they were
only young lads themselves when they demonstrated
their skills to me in the back yard, mesmerising me
with all sorts of tricks. I can still taste the air of old
Cabra West, and those visits are forever embedded in
a place reserved for good memories.

It breaks my heart to think that strangers now live in number 228, that Major is long gone and our time there is just a part of folklore, a dim memory of Dublin in the rare ol' times.

One of the most beautiful ladies that ever existed was my aunt Rosaleen on the mother's side, but alas she was taken far too young. I still have aunties Anne and Marie, who came to visit Clare last year, and they are two rare tickets indeed. A special hello to them. My mom was born of your special family, and I know it made her what she is today. For that, and for her, I am truly grateful.

I am a proper little mommy's boy til this day, much to the disgust of my own siblings, and I look forward to being spoiled rotten for many more years to come. My mother is the most intuitive person I have ever met, even when you believe she must be wrong, way out of the ballpark mistaken in fact, she is invariably proven right. A mother's instinct is a powerful thing, and with Patti Brennan looking out for me, I shall never stray too far from the path.

A Dream

I have to cycle one of those silly little fold up bikes all
the way from Dublin, and I have a flat tyre, not to
mention a dodgy saddle with holes in it, so when it
rains, as it always does, my lovely round arse gets
saturated. I say good luck to my mom and dad, and
begin to pedal down a leafy suburban avenue. I'm
doing alright, it's tough going, but I manage to get to
the N7, the road west, relatively unscathed.
Somewhere around Kildare I come across an
enclosed courtyard, surrounded on all sides by
retirement lodges in various states of dilapidation. I
have to get back to the road, I have work in the
morning, and the pressure is on to get home, but
there is no way out of this little retirement village. So
I try to climb over a few fences with my bike all
folded up, when I get stuck in a mucky garden, and I
am overcome by a state of total agitation.
Then this little old lady opens her door and says in a
kindly way "Are ye stuck, young fella? Bring the bike
in here, through the back, and I'll let ye out the
front." And so I do.
Now I'm in the little old lady's front room. There's
three ancient old boys sat in chairs, and another old
dear. They have a gigantic slobbering pet hound and

a crow, yes a crow, that has been domesticated. It sits on the couch with the dog. The old geezers are very friendly and regale me with stories about the war, the old dears prepare tea and sandwiches to sustain me on my journey. I feel right at home, like I have known these people all my life.

I am reluctant to leave but it's getting dark, the bike is bolloxed, and I have a lot of travelling to do. I thank the folk present, I say goodbye to the dog and the crow and I head out the back with the bike. There, to my utmost astonishment, standing on the doorstep, are two old friends of mine. They shall remain nameless, to protect their identities. One could be loosely described as an ex-girlfriend, and the other, her brother, an ex-jockey who became a successful horse trainer with a big spread in Tipperary.

"What the?" I gasp.

Before I can regain my senses, the ex-girlfriend, who is now the landlady responsible for the entire retirement village, disappears into the house, and much to my helpless horror, begins to evict the unfortunate old folk, the hound, and the bird. The jockey interrupts my state of stunned bewilderment – "Hey Sid, man! What's going on?" he asks, and I explain my current predicament. "No worries, man.

I'll take you as far as Tipp!" So I dump the bike in the back of his big flash motor and off we spin. We get some way down the road when he suddenly announces – "Just taking a detour, Sid." And we drive down a country path until we get to a huge, rambling, estate.

We toddle over to a picnic bench where some bloke is waiting for us. My old pal and this bloke then proceed to negotiate the biggest drugs deal in Irish criminal history.

I ran off to the car, got the old ramshackle bike out of the boot, and flew off as fast as the little wheels would take me.

Just what kind of nutter am I, for heaven's sake? Crows? Dogs? 200 year old geriatrics? Silly little fold up bikes? Gimme a break! I must have made it home, but like my trip home from Mississippi, I guess I'll never know how.

Girls.

When I was nine, and in fourth class in St
Connaire's, I experienced my first real crush. There
had been girls in my childhood in England that I had
been rather taken with, but I was a big boy now, and
this was serious.

Her name was Denise Curran, she was blonder,
vivacious, and in my eyes, a total goddess. Her folks
were friends with my folks, and I would often find
myself in her company. I asked her out, and she said
"Yes. Ok. But I have a boyfriend already." That didn't
seem to matter, and myself and the other boyfriend,
Timmy, agreed to share her. A pre-pubescent rivalry
entailed, and we constantly vied for her attention.
Timmy gave her some lovely flowers one day, and I
was consumed with angst, convinced I was going to
lose her. So that night, I did what any self-respecting
prospective beau would do, I nicked some colouring
pens off my big sister and presented to the blonde
bombshell the next day. She was delighted. She got
stuck into some colouring on the spot, and I had one
up on Timmy.

When I got home, I was confronted by my Mom, and
she was a wee bit peeved. "You stole your sister's
pens, Kevin. You have no choice now, you will have

to get them back!" And so, consumed with regret, knowing full well that Denise would think me a thief and a scoundrel and most likely have done with me altogether, I went into school the next day.

"I've got to get the markers back, Denise. I'm so sorry. I nicked them. Now my sister needs them back." I explained, and much to my surprise, she didn't seem to mind at all. She gave them back, but half were missing, and the rest were all dried up. I went home, gave my sister the remnants of what was once a nice little packet of felt tips, and said "Sorry, what was the best I could do."

Denise naturally began to favour Timmy after that, and my little heart was eventually broken. But my association with girls had begun, and a romantic patter was formed. From then on, I would suffer the slings and arrows to an excruciating extent, never getting it right, and letting so many wonderful prospective partners slip by (as I obsessed about the wrong 'uns) that it really does not bear thinking about. There were many liaisons, too numerous to mention, back in those halcyon days, but I could never get a grip, so to speak, on any of it. It was entirely my fault, in most cases.

I was once attached to a girl who was perfection personified, but I forsook our relationship in favour of hanging about outside the chippy with the lads. I preferred kicking tin cans around to wandering the streets of Shannon with the tall, Mediterranean vision of loveliness.

There was a girl called Susan in Limerick, back in the dark ages. I had charmed her socks off with my English accent, and she had declared her undying love for me. Then my roving eye alighted on her friend and I naturally ended up with neither.

I ignored the right girls, the ones that took a genuine interest, to my eternal regret, and the majority of my dalliances with the opposite sex would invariably lead to one of us being heartbroken. I may have developed a sub conscious aversion to becoming involved as a result of my disastrous forays into half hearted romantic affiliation, because since the dissolution of my ill-fated marriage, I have had one short lived attachment. Liz, the lady that led me to Graceland. Perhaps, deep down, I would prefer to live the life of a monk, because faced with commitment, it seems I'd rather be committed.

These things are not easy to talk about, and I would rather not, but I guess this 'memoir' demands it. I have treated women disgracefully, leading them up the garden path on too many occasions to contemplate. I have no excuse. Do with me as you please, ladies, I deserve it. I have been facetious and uncaring, and on occasions, unforgivably cruel. I have been on the receiving end myself, but that does not make it right, and my apologies, whether they be accepted or not, are heartfelt.

It has been a litany of missed opportunities, the path is littered with Cupid's calamities, but I live in hope. I like to think that I have acquired a fresh perspective. I hope that sobriety and the benefit of hindsight may enable me to move so far forward as to consign the man responsible for so many screw-ups to the garbage bin of history. A little birdie tells me I will not be alone forever, but I am not at liberty to disclose this little birdy's identity until such a time as she is sitting safely on my shoulder.

Reflecting on the Past

"The money pit, in which I dwell, has been further infected with filthy rat droppings and pungent festering slime today.

Paying the sol called maintenance fee on the flat is causing me consternation like nothing I have ever felt. They refuse to maintain the interior of the building, which is falling to pieces, and expect the residents to pay to have some bloke cut the grass outside and little else. There is a hole in my toilet ceiling which leaks brown gunk down the walls at regular intervals.

Although the source of the problem is obviously not contained within my flat, it is still entirely my problem. My state of perplexed agitation is now permanent. I am developing Tourette like tics. Even with the help of my good friend Moira, who occasionally puts on her financial controller hat for my benefit, the figures just don't add up. Even venting my spleen on these pages doesn't temper my apoplexy. The flat's got to go. It does, or I do.

The flat's got to go. It's it, or me."

What a joy it was to read that old passage again. To think that the seemingly impossible situation was resolved in such a spectacular way! How everything fell into place! It was beyond my wildest dreams. Though it may seem a trifling matter to some, it has totally transformed my life. I am no longer driven to drink by my surroundings, and I am preparing for a comfortable retirement in my cosy little abode. I have said it before, but I believe an unseen hand intervened on my behalf, and a gift beyond my imagination was bestowed upon me.

Dad

Some years ago, my teeth were the subject of a
particularly negative diagnosis. According to a female
hygienist with an unfortunately abrupt manner,
there was a need for urgent attention from a
periodontist as they were "rotten beyond salvation".
It appeared I had contracted gingivitis somewhere
along the way, and without treatment, my gnashers
would surely be lost. I was referred to a clinic in
Dublin called The Beacon. An awesome building in
itself, and quite something to behold, as was the
periodontist, a woman of most agreeable
specifications called Rachel. I was then informed that
would need to see Rachel in a professional capacity
ten times over the next six months, that it was going
to cost a veritable fortune, and I should be prepared
for some discomfort.
Being totally unused to driving around Dublin and
possessing an already calamitous sense of direction,
I decided to go visit my folks in Wicklow on the day of
the first appointment, and to impose upon my dad
for a lift to the clinic. He kindly obliged, and off we
went.
The treatment, as advertised, was most unpleasant,
and lasted a full hour and a half. Even the appealing

212

figures of Rachel and her two assistants did little to allay the discomfort. I shall not relate the details of the procedure, suffice to say that it involved pinning my gums back and the employment of a lot of fiendish electronic Gadgets. In short, I did not want to be there. But I most certainly was there, thanks to my dad, who all the time was doing his crossword patiently in the waiting room. It was to be a great comfort to have him there at the end of each ghastly session, as I had roped him in for the long haul by now, and there was much toothy torture ahead.

I can safely say that that dental treatment was a terrible ordeal, and I would recommend scrupulous dental hygiene to anyone, but as I look back, it forms a period of time that I would not swap for anything. I can still see my dad wracking his brains over a crossword clue as I leave the surgery to meet him. I can still feel that consoling arm on my shoulder as steers his senseless, direction free son back to the car park, and I can still hear his voice as we chat on the way home. In the midst of agony, although I was oblivious to it, I was in a perfect place, protected from all the ills of the world, warm, content, with intolerable pain in the jaw, and totally secure.

When they took him from us, they did not only remove his earthly manifestation, they took away his incomparable ability to communicate, and from an entirely selfish point of view, that is what I now miss most. Of course, he still communicated in his own way, and we need to keep the lines open.

My dad must have come home one day from work, with a spring in his step, trusty newspaper in hand, only to find that his little lad, Kevin, the peculiar one, was not waiting at the gate to greet him. I must have moved on from that ritual at some stage, though the process is forever lost in the sands of time. My dad adjusted to the situation fairly quickly, I should think, and just shrugged it off, although he now had no head to tap with his paper. He compensated for that as the years rolled on, by substituting the head tap with another ritual. During my late adolescence and early teens, after I'd come in from a long night's footy, as I lazed on the chair, he would often come up behind me and grab my shoulder in a firm grip. He would squeeze for a good thirty seconds until the sensation I felt hovered between painful and just tolerable, and then he would utter those immortal words, "good man" and go about his business. This little interlude in our lives soon became a permanent fixture, and like the Latin incantations at dinner, it was just a part of everyday life that I took for granted.

My dad was kept going by a veritable pharmacy full of medications in later life. Pills for this, and pills for that, and his heart only operational due to a semi-experimental operation which utilised his mammary gland. He was often unwell, was very frail, and was often very grey about his features.

I often thought he wasn't long for this world, and although I dreaded his demise, to me it always seemed imminent, and I honestly thought I was fully prepared for it. I was wrong of course, and when the unthinkable did happen I was torn asunder. Grief was unbearably physical in its nature, with limbs endlessly aching and a permanent headache. For the first few weeks, something unknown kicks in which protects you from the full realisation of the event. A protective cocoon of sorts, which is part shock and part self-preservation.

I went through these natural mourning processes, and was able to finally complete the procedure after Pascal had sent me a wonderful tribute to my dad. He used very simple terms, but summed him up perfectly. The floodgates opened, and after almost a month, the full realisation finally dawned on me. It was necessary, and supremely cleansing for the soul. A couple of days after the text, I was lying in bed, fretting a little, wide awake, and as sober as a judge.

I was in fact, enduring a sort of hypersensitivity due to lack of sleep, but my mind was clear, and I was just making the most of the rest, as you do. I lay on my stomach, and just contemplated a while.

Then it happened! I felt that familiar grip on my shoulder. The unmistakable hand of my father. He squeezed for thirty seconds or so, and I knew it could not be anything else. It was not a spasm, or some form of strange muscular aberration, if it were, I would have recognised it as such. No! This was my dad's hand, beyond doubt.

I lay there for the full thirty seconds as he went thought that very same squeezing procedure of yore. I wasn't shocked, I wasn't surprised, I just took it in my stride. It didn't seem unusual at the time, I was 100% certain it was him, and that was all there was to it. Seconds afterwards, I heard my own voice say "That just happened. You were not imagining it. It was not a dream. You are wide awake. Never, ever, forget how real this is" and I no hesitancy in relating this story, as I am convinced as I ever was. I need not tell you, I would never treat such a subject flippantly, and I am not given to superstitious mumbo jumbo.

This was my father's reassuring hand, and at that moment my grief turned into celebration at his continued existence.

Metaphysics

I am aware of the implications of what I am saying. I
am stating with absolute certainty that my dad's
departure from this world was merely a step into
another realm. I am aware of the ramifications,
because I have thought about it every day since.
There is an afterlife. Do not dismiss this as the
ravings of a lunatic. What I felt was real, and could
not be mistaken for anything else. I felt his grip, and
since then I have been blissfully aware of his guiding
hand in my life. Since that moment, a great anxiety
has been lifted from me. I fear nothing. My feet
finally found their place, and I am transformed.
I try not to dwell on it from a religious point of view,
as my dad was a practicing Catholic, and I worry
that non-adherence to that doctrine might ultimately
prove costly to me! I see it as a spiritual event,
nothing less, nothing more, but an event that has
totally changed my outlook on life for ever more.
I didn't listen to my dad enough when he was on this
Earth, but irony of all ironies, he finally got through
to me from beyond this mortal coil of ours, and as I
sit here, I know he guides my pen. I was not privy to
a sudden enlightening illumination, and I do not
know what the afterlife entails, or indeed whether we

are all to be treated to one. For all I know, it could be just a chosen few. I do know what happened that night, however, and I am under no illusions about it. The shoulder grip was a uniquely recognisable thing. The pressure begins between the thumb and forefinger, and travels down along the other fingers, there is a tight squeeze involving all five fingers at once, and then the pressure travels back towards the thumb and forefinger again. It would make me wriggle about in discomfort for a second or two, which from my da's point of view was obviously the point of the exercise, and then equilibrium of the shoulders was happily restored.

I am anxious to impress upon anyone still reading this that this shoulder grip could not be mistaken for anything else. Try it at home! Have someone perform the operation on you. It is an entirely external sensation as the fingers begin to grip, and then it causes inner spasms. This is precisely what I felt, and it was not just a fleeting sensation. It lasted long enough for me to be aware of what I was while it was happening, and although I know now that it had all sorts of cosmic connotations, at the time, like I said, it just seemed absolutely natural and perfectly plausible.

Whether or not I am believed, I am happy to have recorded this for posterity. I do not want to cause offense, and to anyone who feels I am treating a sacred subject in a facetious way, I apologise. Many would say I was having a magic mushroom flashback, or that my subconscious brought about this miraculous happening in an attempt to ease my suffering. But it really wasn't like that, and I can only ask that people accept what I am saying at face value. There are many folk who will readily accept this, and it is a great comfort to me to know that. To the others I say... well... time will tell, my friends, time will tell.

It is easy to see why I was reluctant to include this episode, as it leaves me open to all sorts of reactions and I am not sure I could cope with any of them, whether they be positive or negative. I do know that since it happened a very positive change has taken place deep within me. It appears that I am now armed with a certain knowledge. Nothing can phase me now. Physical ailments and the pain related to them are mere transient earthbound afflictions, and being aware of something so much deeper enables me to treat them as such.

I don't like to use such labels, and humanity has the irritating habit of attaching names to things we cannot comprehend, but 'God' is as good a name as any other to describe a supreme being of sorts, and my experience certainly seems to indicate the existence of one. This is an intensely Earth shattering revelation, and my limited mind has yet to come to grips with it.

As I may have mentioned, my dad's faith was unshakable, and perhaps it was the nature of his beliefs, and their inherent strengths, that brought him to a world beyond this one. By the same token, perhaps I am doomed, as I remain resolutely agnostic in my outlook, despite everything. Religious fundamentalism is not for me, but I am now completely convinced that this life is a stepping stone to another existence. We can only hope it will be a good one, free of the trials and tribulations we endure on Earth. The beatings, the insecurities, the discrimination, the failed relationships, the hangovers, the violent episodes, the brushes with the law, the loneliness, the isolation, incapacitating backache, the endless and desperate longing for sensual involvement, all of these things are rendered suddenly irrelevant and have been replaces with something that goes beyond hope. It is an absolute certainty. Our ultimate redemption is assured.

Soon it will be three years since my outlook was changed so dramatically, and I am grateful for the chance to commit it to record while it is still fresh in my memory.

My family will no doubt think I have finally lost my marbles, it has been on the cards for many years after all, but this is something that happened.

Heaven knows why it happened to me, but I cannot alter the fact that it happened, regardless of how it is subsequently interpreted.

All I can do is tell it like it is and leave myself at your mercy.

Fin

So, in order to stay off booze for Christmas, acquire
yourself a book from a friendly receptionist who
bears no resemblance to any Australian soap star,
living or dead, p-p-p-pick up a pen, and let the
nonsense flow. It need not resemble literature, as
this effort demonstrates, but who said it needs to?
Pretty soon you will have a work in progress.
Invisible forces will then begin to press you into
further work. Long lost memories will begin to jostle
in your noggin, all anxious to be included.
The pen will take on a life of its own, at times, a
phenomena I like to refer to as 'auto-writing'. An
example of which is what I am writing at this very
moment. I have no idea where this is coming from, or
where it's going. I trust in the boundless tolerance of
the potential reader, safe in the knowledge that he or
she is not casting too critical an eye over
proceedings, and in the hope that this exercise is
being perused in a non-judgemental fashion. It is
intended as a long letter to my friends, and I
sincerely hope they receive it in good time. I believe I
am a man without enemies, but I know there are
those that will scoff at the contents of this
manuscript and attempt to discredit me. To them I

say, life is too short, I only did it for a laugh, and if you don't like it you can lump it.

To my friends I say "Hi friends. I have written a little something for you. I am going to give it to my good son, Shaybo (nobody fucking calls me that, not even my dad. – Ed), and he has promised to edit along the way. I am hoping that after his input has rendered it somewhat comprehensible it will become a palatable piece of prose." Oh! And "I sincerely hope that I am not regarded as someone who pretentiously believes himself to be a writer. I know my limitations, and remember, the pen for the most part has directed itself. So if you want to sue someone, sue the pen."

We never did get to talk about my time as 'The Giant Jockey of Suckley, Worcestershire" but perhaps we'll get around to it someday. This has been an unbelievably cathartic experience for me. Although it came about quite by accident. I was only chancing my arm when I asked dear old Beany for a diary, and I had no idea what would ensue.

I still have no idea of what ensued, but it is a creation of sorts and it has gone some way toward compensation for the loss of my giant life's opus. It was a joy to share memories of Basil, and I am delighted to have kept his spirit somehow alive. There are so many others who I barely alluded to, all of whom played crucial roles in my life. I wanted to spare their blushes for the most part, for I well up with sentiment when I think of them. How blessed I have been by association with you all, and you know who you are.

Finally, thank you Dad, for your guiding hand in life, and on into infinity.

Made in the USA
Middletown, DE
17 May 2018